GREYSTONE'S
Creative Hands

EDITOR

Beverley Hilton

GREYSTONE PRESS/NEW YORK · TORONTO · LONDON

Volume 1

© Fratelli Fabri Editore, Milan 1966, 1967
Marshall Cavendish Limited 1970, 1971, 1972, 1973, 1975
Manufactured in the United States of America
Library of Congress Catalog Card No. 75-8338

Much of the material contained herein has
previously been published in separate parts
under the title Golden Hands.

Contents

Collector's Piece
The Bradford Carpet 20
Snowy Owls 70
Checkerboard Panel 90
Crochet: Basic Wardrobe
Tunic suit for a tiny tot 44
Top and pants for a toddler 104
Crochet Know-how
Introduction to crochet 10
Singles and doubles 12
Lots of new stitches to try 46
Increase or decrease 66
Making neat work of joins 86
Crochet a vest in squares 106
Dressmaking
The secret of successful dressmaking 28
The basic tools for successful sewing 30
How to measure up 32
Start with a pop-over pinafore 34
Coming to grips with your figure 54
Fabric and design 56
Prints and patterns 57
Pick your poncho 58
Theme and variations on a simple skirt 76
Pattern making from a graph 78
Preparing to sew the skirt 96
Embroidery
Yarns, frames and needles 14
Stitch families and pattern darning 16
Don't ignore the simple line stitches 48
Transferring your design 68
Planning a color scheme 88
Straight stitches and knots 100
Fashion Flair
Frog fastening 38
Pull-on jersey hat 60
Quick-sew cover-up 80
Peasant-style bolero 110
Fringing
Simple knot 26
Lattice fringe and tassels 52
Home Sewing
Make a mitred tablecloth 50
Knitting: Basic Wardrobe
Knit a classic sweater for a man 64
Striped pullovers 84
Knitting Know-how
Introduction to knitting 6
Choose your casting on method 8
Meet the basic stitches 42
Binding off and the slipped stitch 62
Making patterns from purl and knit 82
Binding off invisibly 108
Needle-made Lace
Flounce and filigree 94
Needlepoint
Canvas, yarns and needles 18
One stitch and a batch of buttons 22
What's in a sampler? 72
More stitches for your sampler 92
Pattern Library
Floral embroidery 41
Cross-stitch alphabet 61
Cross-stitch design 81
Rediscovering the Gentle Arts 24
Take care
Paper pattern sizes 40
Toy Making
Honeybun the bunny 74

GREYSTONE'S

Creative Hands

GREYSTONE PRESS/NEW YORK · TORONTO · LONDON

Creative Hands

Your guide to creative knitting, dressmaking, home sewing, mending, care and altering, embroidery, crochet, canvas work, macramé, toymaking, tatting, needle made lace . . . and saving money.

If you've never picked up a needle, **Creative Hands** will show you how to make a wonderful wardrobe—starting right from scratch. Because the chapters follow one another in a logical, sensible way, each new article you make teaches you a new skill. Yet our designer's flair for fascinating subjects means this is one course which is never, *never* dull!

Creative Hands will help you save money, too. You'll save by making exciting and practical clothes that you used to consider 'too hard'. And you'll save by making many things for your home—cushions, curtains, toys and rugs which will delight you and your family. Also, **Creative Hands** is your key to the world of high fashion—without the price tag!

These illustrations show just a few of the things you'll learn to make through **Creative Hands**. And remember, it is the most complete knitting, dressmaking and needlecraft guide ever published—books which will be a source of pleasure for many years to come.

If you're already a needlewoman, **Creative Hands** will show you new horizons. How to give your garments a better fit, a more professional finish. How to use techniques you've probably never tried. How to adapt basic patterns to suit fashion's newest edict—or your own fancy. How to develop your own designing skills and creative abilities.

Creative Hands will also bring you beyond traditional needlework and help you become a complete craftsman. Special craft entries include: Candlemaking • Beadweaving • Enameling • Arrangements with pressed and preserved flowers • Paper sculpture • Tie and dye • Making beaded jewelry • Lampshade making • Suede and leatherwork.

How to use Creative Hands

Creative Hands is an up-to-date guide to enjoying the beautiful new materials, aids, techniques, and exciting designs of modern creative needlecraft. This is a book for the woman who likes to improve on present talents or discover new ones —for the beginner and experienced needlewoman alike. It's for any woman who wants to make clothes with flair and individuality or to create good-looking decorative furnishings for her home.

The key to doing anything successfully is clear know-how and inspiration—with these two ingredients, all things are possible! The following pages set out to make the art of creating things thoroughly satisfying. They're full of just the kind of know-how that makes projects work on the first try, saves time and money and sets you to thinking of a hundred different possibilities.

The complete book is made up of many strands. Some of these, like Dressmaking, and the Basic Wardrobe of Knitting and Crochet, continue right through the book. Other strands, like Home Sewing, Rug-making, Patchwork and Needlepoint, are run in rotation. To make it easy to find your way around, we have given each strand a key symbol (some are shown below), and each symbol carries its own chapter number.

But this book isn't just about knitting, or even sewing. Every aspect of needlework—dress designing; mending and altering; making slip covers and curtains; as well as the creative skills of macrame, tatting and embroidery—is covered, so that with each chapter you can discover something new, become a little more expert. The whole of Creative Hands is designed so that you can use it as a course in any subject you choose and, at the same time, as an encyclopedic book of reference to techniques and patterns.

DRESSMAKING. Elisa Boness has made sumptuous clothes for aristocrats, jet-set socialites and diplomats' wives. She trained in Germany, worked in England, and then became professional dressmaker for Vogue promotions. Her triumphs have included dazzling wardrobes for a reigning Miss World, for top actresses appearing both on the stage and on television, and a dashing new uniform for an international airline.

Elisa advises home dressmakers always to adapt all fashions to their own figure type and way of life. She advocates investment in a good full-length mirror, and ruthless criticism of one's figure, from the back as well as the front. She also feels that most young women don't spend enough time or money on their wardrobe, when for just a few dollars more and a really carefully planned selection, their clothes could look absolutely stunning.

Jo Springer began using her hands at the age of five and is still at it. She insists that the only craft that she hasn't tried is glass blowing! After attending the University of Chicago, she graduated from Washington University in St. Louis, where she became an occupational therapist. As the youngest female captain in the U.S. Army during World War II, she trained all the occupational therapy assistants used in Army hospitals.

After working on a graduate degree in Fine Arts Education at Columbia University Teachers' College, Jo spent over five years in an editorial capacity at Woman's Day magazine. This was followed by a stint in fashion public relations. Finally, she returned full time to her first love—the designing of crafts and needlework for various publications, and the writing of material related to the field. Her books include "Creative Needlework" and "Betty Crocker's Pleasures of Crewel."

An exposure to knitting and crocheting at an early age instilled in Pat Boyle the desire to pursue these creative handcrafts. Her first professional involvement was as an apprentice in a design studio where she absorbed the diverse intricacies of the crafts. She then joined Vogue Knitting where she held the position of associate editor and managing editor, during which time she proved to be an invaluable design contributor and consultant. Her seven years as editor-in-chief of Vogue Knitting were dedicated to forecasting fashion in the yarn industry and presenting the public with fresh designs and 'how to' directions.

Pat's creative energy is presently channeled into free-lance designing. At the same time she is very involved in introducing and teaching handcrafts to young people. She is fascinated when watching their young minds grasp the techniques, and delighted with their creative accomplishments.

Dress-making

If you are new to one field or another, you can use Creative Hands as a course because each chapter takes you step-by-step in the clearest possible way through every technique you need to know. In no time at all you will be able to sew, knit and crochet all the garments featured.

If you are an experienced needlewoman you can use Creative Hands as a comprehensive book of reference. It offers you specialized dressmaking and design skills; a whole library of beautiful patterns for needlepoint, embroidery and the gentle arts; and dozens of finely tailored garment patterns to knit, sew and crochet. These include adorable babies' clothes, tough children's things, smart fashions for teenage girls and boys, lots of pretty designs for yourself and handsome ideas for the man in your life. There are other chapters which are specially devoted to making wedding, maternity and layette garments.

The 'Take Care!' chapters are the extra-important ones on how to keep your wardrobe and home in good order. These give money-saving information on how to mend a collar on a shirt, alter last year's dress, or repair a disastrous tear in a garment. These chapters also cover the washing and care of new fabrics, plus a complete guide to stain removal.

So—if you long to emulate a friend who crocheted her own evening dress; or know you could be saving money by making individual clothes for yourself and your children; or would like to do a better job of sewing your own curtains; or if you long to decorate your home by giving it a very personal embroidered picture—then this is your book.

Creative Hands brings together a widely experienced and imaginative group of consultants, each one a recognized expert in his or her field (you can see a few of them on these pages). The whole team hopes you will enjoy Creative Hands and find it helpful and inspiring for many years to come.

KNITTING AND CROCHET. Rae Compton is known for her warm personality as much as for her expertise. She went to art school in Edinburgh, Scotland, and then almost by chance, while at home looking after her two small children, sent a 'test piece' baby's bonnet to Vogue. Much to her surprise she received a telegram offering to buy the pattern! Soon she was forging ahead with knitting designs, and was asked to design the layette for Princess Margaret's first baby. Later she became editor of Vogue's knitting publications, and now designs for top yarn manufacturers.

Rae is eager to see knitting standards raised, and lectures upon this subject to many women's groups. She finds her audiences hungry for new information, and that, too often, home-knitters are only using familiar ideas, when there are so many methods to be discovered. You'll find some in Creative Hands!

EMBROIDERY AND NEEDLE-POINT. Eileen Lowcock finds modern embroidery constantly inspiring. She deplores the fact that the work of so many accomplished home embroiderers is still restricted by out-of-date designs and unimaginative subjects, when there are so many more exciting possibilities to explore. Her aim is to arouse a feeling for the use of design and color in anybody who is interested in embroidery. She wants to encourage people who formerly discounted the craft to see that it really is a creative art which reflects modern living every bit as much as fashion in dress and architecture.

Eileen studied design for 5 years while at art school. She ran her own dressmaking business for 10 years, while also teaching in adult education classes. She then became the Technical Crafts Adviser for Britain's largest nationwide association for women.

TATTING. Mary Konior grew up in a family interested in hand crafts and became expert at tatting when very young, so it was a natural step for her to become a teacher of arts and crafts. She finds that traditional skills, such as tatting, which were immensely popular in the nineteenth and early twentieth centuries, lost their popularity in the period between the World Wars. But Mary has found that her teaching is now very much in demand, especially by younger people who are eager to learn a somewhat different craft. She finds that this very delicate lace, made with a shuttle, can add some lovely borders to all sorts of linens, bridal veils, shawls, or scarves. Or, if you're very patient, make a tablecloth.

NET EMBROIDERY. Ann Mary Pilcher teaches needlework all over Britain, in courses organized by local branches of the Embroiderers' Guild and various women's organizations. Ann is an avid collector of antique and foreign needlework, and one of her prize possessions is a lovely embroidered linen Georgian waistcoat, complete with handmade buttons. She advises all readers who have similar collections to consult an expert about cleaning and repairs, since so much antique work is very fragile.

Her designs are inspired by many unusual subjects, such as primitive sculpture, and she is constantly on the lookout for new ways to combine traditional designs with modern materials.

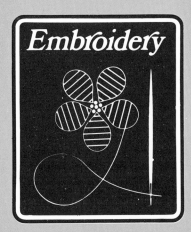

5

New ways with fashion knitting

Hand knitting is one of the most popular fashion crafts these days. New dyes, fibers, metallic yarns, mixed yarns and beautiful nubby textures all lend themselves well to the fluid, flexible quality of hand knitting. What is more, techniques from different countries are now circulating internationally, so that there is a wealth of new information available. For beginners, these Knitting Know-how chapters present a clear guide to the basic techniques. For more experienced knitters, there are many clever, little-known techniques like the invisible casting-on method in Knitting Know-how 2, a range of garments in the Basic Wardrobe chapters and hints on how to do your own designing.

The Tools of the Trade

- ☐ A metal or wooden ruler
- ☐ Scissors
- ☐ Darning needles
- ☐ Rustless steel pins
- ☐ Stitch holder (like a large safety pin, to hold stitches not in use)
- ☐ Row counter
- ☐ Knitting needle gauge to check correct needle size
- ☐ Cloth or plastic bag in which to keep knitting clean
- ☐ Iron and ironing board with pad
- ☐ Cotton cloths suitable for use when pressing

Know your needles

Modern knitting needles are usually made of lightweight coated metal or of plastic, and should always be kept in good condition. Bent, scratched or uneven needles will spoil the evenness of your knitting, and should be discarded.

For 'straight' knitting—that is, knitting worked backwards and forwards on two needles—needles with knobs at one end are advisable, as they lessen the possibility of dropped stitches, which is frustrating to the most even-tempered knitter.

For socks, gloves, certain types of sweaters, and any garment which is knitted 'around'—that is, in a circle instead of straight—a set of four or more needles is used, pointed at both ends. A flexible circular needle is used for some designs for seamless circular garments, like skirts. The effect is the same as dividing the work among three or more needles, but the work is much easier to handle and one avoids having loose stitches where the needles join.

Needle sizes

With any knitted design, you will need a specified number in a knitting needle. Here is a chart of the American and British sizes. As you will see, with American sizes the lower the number, the smaller the diameter of the needle, whereas with the British sizes the reverse is true.

Knitting Needle Sizes	
American	British and Canadian
15	000
13	00
12	0
11	1
10½	2
10	3
9	4
8	5
7	6
6	7
5	8
4	9
3	10
2	11
1	12
0	13
00	14

Yarns and ply

Yarn is the word used to describe any spun thread, whether it is fine or thick. It may be a natural fiber like wool, cotton, linen, silk, angora, or mohair—or a man-made fiber like Acrilan, Orlon, nylon or rayon.

When choosing a yarn, you will come across the word ply. This indicates the number of spun single threads that have been twisted together. Each single thread can be spun to any thickness so that a simple reference to the ply does not necessarily determine the thickness of the finished yarn, although the terms 2-ply, 3-ply and 4-ply are often used to mean yarn of a recognized thickness. The following ply classification is broadly applicable to the majority of hand-knitting yarns whether made from wool, man-made fibers or blends of both.

Baby yarns are usually made from the higher quality yarns, and are available in 3-ply and 4-ply.

2-ply, 3-ply and 4-ply yarns may consist of wool, wool and man-made fiber blends, or 100% man-made fiber.

Sport Weight yarns are usually 4-ply yarns in which the single strands are about ½ the thickness of knitting worsted.

Knitting Worsted yarns are the most widely used of all yarns, and are usually made from four spun single threads (although there are exceptions to this), twisted together to produce hard-wearing yarns.

Bulky yarns can either be 2-ply, 3-ply or 4-ply. They are spun like any other basic yarn but each strand is of a heavier weight.

Dress yarns are usually novelty yarns, spun in a completely different manner to the basic yarns in order to create more interesting and unusual textures. They are generally not designated according to ply.

Very important!

Since there is no official standardization, yarns marketed by different firms often vary in thickness and in yardage.

If you cannot obtain the yarn suggested in the directions, or have set your heart on something else, it is possible to use other yarn, provided you can obtain the same gauge as given in the pattern. Always buy sufficient yarn at one time so that all the yarn used is from the same dye lot. Yarn from a different dye lot may vary very slightly, but even the slightest difference can cause an unsightly line across your work, marring the whole garment.

Your success depends on gauge

To make any design successfully it is absolutely vital that you obtain the same gauge as given in the directions. This point cannot be over emphasised!

This means that you must obtain the same number of stitches to the inch and *also* the same number of rows to the inch as the designer obtained.

To test your knit gauge, cast on 20 sts with the needles that are specified. Work even for 3 inches in given pattern. Bind off and press swatch lightly. Pin down on paper. With a ruler, measure across one inch, then down one inch, counting the number of stitches and rows to the inch. If you have more stitches to the inch than given in the directions, use a larger needle. If you have fewer stitches and rows to the inch than given, use a smaller needle. Continue to work up swatches until the gauge is correct. Testing the gauge not only applies to the beginner but also to the experienced knitter.

A few minutes spent on this preparation lays the foundation for a successful garment. If it is overlooked, a great deal of work may be undertaken before the error in size is realized. Even half a stitch too many or too few, although seemingly little, amounts to nine stitches too many or too few on the back of a 34 inch sweater. This can mean the completed sweater is 2 inches too large or too small. Once you have worked your gauge swatch, lay it on a flat surface and pin it down. Place a tape measure on your knitting and mark out one inch with pins. Count the number of stitches between the two pins very carefully.

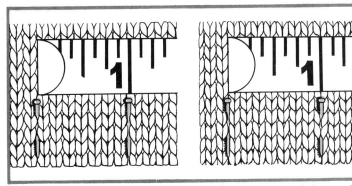

▲ *The inches are marked out with pins, left, showing 7 stitches to the inch: right, measuring between the pins gives 7½ stitches to the inch*

▼ *The gauge swatch is pinned into a perfect square, ready to measure*

Abbreviations

Here is a list of knitting terms which are usually printed in a shortened form.

In some designs it is necessary to use a special abbreviation applicable to that design only.

In such a case the abbreviation will be explained at the point where it is first used, or placed in a clear note before the beginning of the directions.

beg	=beginning
dec	=decrease by working 2 stitches together
dp	=double-pointed
in	=inch(es)
inc	=increase by working into front and back of stitch
K	=knit
LH	=left hand
P	=purl
patt	=pattern
psso	=pass slip stitch over
rem	=remaining
rep	=repeat
RH	=right hand
RS	=right side
sl 1K	=slip 1 knitwise
sl 1P	=slip 1 purlwise
st(s)	=stitch(es)
st st	=stockinette stitch
tog	=together
WS	=wrong side
yo	=yarn over
yo as to K	=bring yarn under right-hand needle to front, then over needle to back, then you are ready to knit the next st
yo as to P	=wind yarn around right-hand needle once and yarn is then in position to p the next st
yrn	=yarn round needle
ytb	=yarn to back
ytf	=yarn to front
*	=(asterisk) repeat directions following * as many extra times as directed
[ ]	=[brackets] numbers set in brackets refer to alternate sizes
( )	=(parentheses) when parentheses are used to show repeats, work the directions in ( ) as many times as specified. "(K1, p1) 3 times" means to do what is inside ( ) 3 times in all
multiple	=multiple in pattern stitches means the number of stitches necessary to complete one whole pattern. If the pattern given is 4 sts, the number of stitches on needle should be evenly divisible by 4. If the pattern reads "multiple of 4 sts plus 1" then 1 extra stitch is required in addition to the multiple of 4.

Choose your casting on method

The first step in knitting is casting on, which provides the first row of loops, or stitches, on the needle. There are various ways of casting on, each with its own appropriate use, and here, the two most popular methods are outlined. Also, the intriguing 'invisible' European method, which may be new to many experienced knitters, is introduced.

The Thumb method (using only one needle) is an excellent way to begin most garments, since it gives an elastic and therefore hard-wearing edge. On the other hand, the Two needle (or English cable) version is necessary when you want to cast on extra stitches during the knitting itself, for instance for a buttonhole or a pocket.

The 'invisible' European method of casting on gives the fashionably flat-hemmed effect of a machine-made garment. It is a flexible, strong finish which can hold ribbon or elastic and is very useful for designs which need casings.

The scarf on this page uses the Thumb method; later issues will present garments that are to be made with both the 'invisible' method of casting on and the English cable method.

Pick your own scarf color, then follow instructions on the facing page

Thumb method— using one needle

To cast on make a slip loop in the yarn about a yard from the end. (This length varies with the number of stitches to be cast on—allow about ½in for each stitch in medium and about 1in for each stitch in heavier yarn. A guide to the length required is—the width of the piece of knitting to be cast on, multiplied by three.)

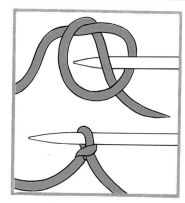

1. Slip loop on to needle which should be held in the right hand.

Two needle method— or English cable

To cast on make a slip loop in the yarn as given for the Thumb method, at least three inches from the end. It is not necessary to try and estimate the length of yarn required to cast on the number of stitches with this method, as you will be working from the ball of yarn. Slip this loop onto the left-hand knitting needle.

1. Insert right-hand needle into loop holding yarn in right hand and wind yarn under and over the needle.

Invisible casting-on method

Even if you are an experienced knitter, you'll be delighted to discover the many uses to which this marvelous new technique lends itself.
1. Using a contrast yarn, which is later removed, and the Thumb method, cast on half the number of stitches required, plus one. Now using the correct yarn for the garment, begin the ribbing.

1st row. K1, *ytf, K1, rep from * to end.
2nd row. K1, *ytf, sl 1, ytb, K1, rep from * to end.
3rd row. Sl 1, *ytb, K1, ytf, sl 1, rep from * to end.

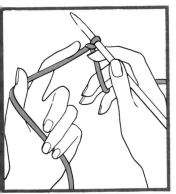

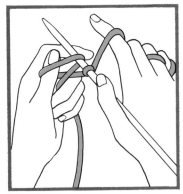

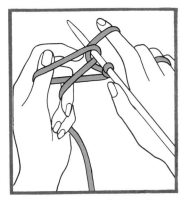

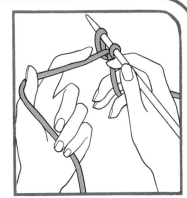

2. Working with the short length of yarn in the left hand, pass this round the left thumb.

3. Insert the point of the needle under the loop on the thumb, and hook forward the long end of yarn from the ball.

4. Wind yarn under and over the needle and draw through loop, leaving stitch on needle.

5. Tighten stitch on needle, noting that yarn is round thumb ready for next stitch.
6. Repeat steps 3-5 for required number of stitches.

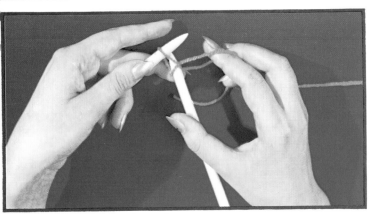

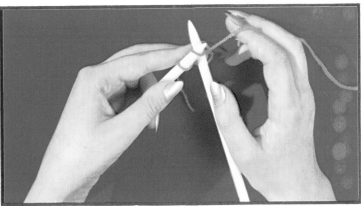

2. Draw the new loop through the first loop on left-hand needle thus forming a second loop. Pass newly made loop onto the left-hand needle.

3. Place point of right-hand needle between two loops on left-hand needle and wind yarn under and over the right-hand needle point and draw this new loop through between the two stitches on the left-hand needle. Slip this loop on to left-hand needle.

4. Repeat steps described in paragraph 3 between last 2 stitches on left-hand needle until the required number of stitches have been cast on.

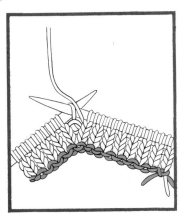

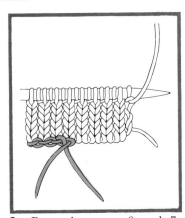

Repeat 2nd and 3rd rows once more.
6th row. K1, *P1, K1, rep from * to end.
7th row. P1, *K1, P1, rep from * to end.

2. Repeating rows 6 and 7, continue in ribbing for the required depth. Pick out the contrasting yarn. The ribbing should appear to be running under the edge.

Beginners — knit yourself a scarf

If you have never knitted before start with one of the scarves on the opposite page. After chapter 4 it will be ready to wear.

Sizes: Woman's is 12½in × 72 in; Child's is 7½in × 50in. Directions are given for the woman's scarf. Changes for the child's are in parentheses.

Materials: 4-Ply Knitting Yarn, or any other yarn that gives the same gauge, 4-oz skeins, 3 for woman's; 2 for child's. No. 10 knitting needles or Canadian No. 3.

Gauge: 4 stitches = 1in.

To begin: Using the thumb method of casting on, cast on 50 (30) stitches.
(For directions on how to knit these scarves, see Knitting Know-how 3.)

Get hooked on crochet

Crochet is a most important look in the world of fashion today. It works up very quickly so it is of particular interest to the woman whose time is very limited and who would like to add crochet designs to her wardrobe or her home. Once the three basic steps have been mastered, there are dozens of patterns for one to work with, like the traditional American Granny squares pictured on the opposite page (see chapter 5 on how to make these squares). One useful feature about these squares is that they are so easy to carry around—in a handbag even! They can be worked separately and then joined together to make anything from a bedspread to a shawl or a vest.

Although crochet is simple, it provides marvelously crisp textures and color effects, which makes it ideal for heavy or unusual garments. Fringed shawls, ponchos, tote bags, and even belts made in crochet are so very easy to do and, in turn, do so much to liven up your wardrobe.

If you knit, you will probably notice that anything that you crochet tends to use more yarn than a design that is knitted. However, because the crochet rows are deeper than the knitted rows, you will be able to finish the work in a much shorter time, whether it's a man's tie, an elegant evening dress or a cosy afghan.

Equipped for action

Crochet hooks are made of steel, bone, plastic or aluminum. Steel crochet hooks range in size from number 00, the largest, to number 14, the smallest. Bone, plastic, and aluminum hooks range in size from B (number 1), the smallest, to K (number 10½), the largest.

Below is a list of sizes for bone, plastic and aluminum hooks; Millimeter sizes are given in parentheses.

K	(7.00)	F	(4.00)
J	(6.00)	E	(3.50)
I	(5.50)	D	(3.00)
H	(5.00)	C	(2.50)
G	(4.50)	B	(2.00)

The following tools will also be helpful:
- ☐ Metal or wooden ruler
- ☐ Scissors
- ☐ Rustless pins
- ☐ Sewing needle with large eye, and some with blunt points
- ☐ Iron and ironing board with pad
- ☐ Cloth or plastic bag to keep work clean
- ☐ Cloths for pressing

Take care with yarn

All types of yarns are suitable for crochet—whether thick or thin, natural or man-made fibers—not only the fine cottons or linens used for the more traditional types of fine crochet.

If you are not absolutely certain that you can achieve the same gauge, then it is wisest to buy the brand of yarn specified in the directions. A different brand may make it difficult for you to obtain the correct measurements. But as in knitting, if you can obtain the number of stitches and rows given in the directions, then you can use any other yarn that gives the same number of stitches and rows to the inch.

Always buy sufficient quantity to complete the garment so that all the yarn comes from the same dye lot. Another dye lot may vary very slightly and cause unwanted stripes. When working with balls of crochet cotton, always use the end from the center of the ball as it flows more smoothly when being worked.

The importance of gauge

Gauge is one of the most important factors towards successful work. If you do not get the number of stitches and rows to one inch that are stated in the directions your garment cannot have the correct measurements when completed.

Beginners should practice trying to obtain the correct gauge, but if it proves very difficult to obtain while trying to hold hook and yarn comfortably, then different hook sizes should be tried.

Before beginning a garment, work a four inch square. If you find you have fewer stitches to the inch than given, then use a smaller hook; if on measuring you find you have too many stitches to the inch, then you must use a larger hook.

Common abbreviations

(Complicated abbreviations will be explained as they occur.)

alt	=alternate	rem	=remaining
beg	=beginning	rep	=repeat
ch	=chain(s)	rnd	=round
cl	=cluster	sc	=single crochet
dc	=double crochet	RS	=right side
dec	=decrease	sdc	=short double crochet
gr	=group		
hdc	=half double crochet	sp	=space
		ss	=slip stitch
inc	=increase	st(s)	=stitches
in	=inch	WS	=wrong side
patt	=pattern	yoh	=yarn over hook

N.B. It should be noted that yoh is the first movement in crochet and forms an important part of every stitch.

An asterisk * means to repeat directions following the * as many extra times as specified.

Repeat instructions in parentheses as many times as specified. For example: (5ch, dc into next dc) 5 times, means to make all that is in brackets 5 times.

Multiple means the number of stitches necessary to complete one pattern. If the pattern is 4 sts, the number of chains should be evenly divisible by 4. If the pattern reads "multiple of 4 sts plus 1" then an extra chain stitch is required in addition to the multiple of 4.

How to begin

The beginning of crochet is to make a slip loop in the yarn and place it on the hook.

1. To make a slip loop: Wrap yarn around first and second fingers of left hand. Insert hook under front loop and draw the back loop through to form a new loop, slipping it off fingers and transferring it to the hook. Pull the loop tight.

2. Holding yarn and hook: Before making a chain, which is the next step, it is necessary to know how to hold the hook and the yarn correctly.

The hook is held in your right hand in the same way as you hold a pen or pencil. This means you hold it between thumb and first finger, letting the hook rest against the second finger, which controls it in moving through the stitches.

The left hand is used to hold the work as it is made, and to control the yarn from the ball. Control the yarn by passing it over the first and second fingers of the left hand, then under the third finger and around the little finger—letting the yarn flow loosely.

3. Chain stitch: Hold the stitch you have made between thumb and first finger of left hand.

Pass hook from left to right under the yarn over your left hand fingers, and over the hook. This is called 'yarn over hook' (yoh) and is a most important part of all stitches. Draw yarn through loop on hook. This makes 1 chain stitch (ch).

4. Repeat this step until you have as many chain stitches as you need, being careful to move your left-hand thumb and finger up the chain to hold the stitch you have just made. Practice making chains until you can hold hook and yarn comfortably.

5. To fasten off: Cut yarn about six inches from work. Thread loose end through the one remaining loop on the hook and pull it tightly.

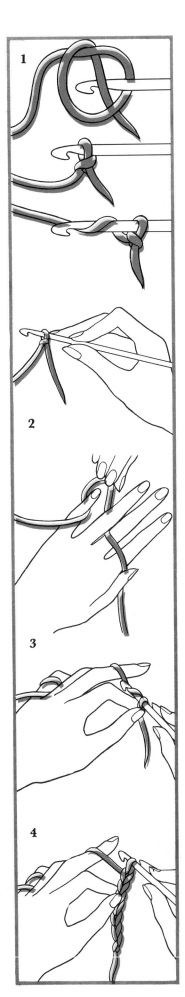

Singles and doubles

To begin crocheting, make a chain and then work back along that chain with your chosen stitch. The top edge of this row forms a new chain base for the next row. Remember to pick up the top two loops of the chain formed by the previous row, unless otherwise instructed. This creates an even surface.

Chain stitch (ch)

Make a loop on hook, * wrap yarn over hook and draw yarn through the preceding loop; repeat from * for the desired length. Each loop is counted as one chain stitch.

Single crochet (sc)

Make a chain the required length.
1st row. Skip the first two chains. * Insert hook in next chain, yarn over hook, draw through loop (2 loops on hook), yarn over hook, and draw through both loops (1 loop on hook). This makes one single crochet. Repeat from * to end of chain. Turn.
2nd row. Ch2, skip first single crochet.* Insert hook through next single crochet (picking up both loops), yarn over hook, draw loop through (2 loops on hook), yarn over hook, draw loop through both loops on hook (1 loop on hook), repeat from * in every single crochet stitch, working last single crochet into turning chain on previous row. Turn.
Repeat 2nd row until the work measures the required length. End off.
Occasionally check the number of stitches at the end of each row, to make sure you have worked the full number of stitches that you had at the end of the second row.

Double stitch (dc)

Make the required length of chain plus 3 turning chains.
1st row. Skip first 3 chains, * yarn over hook, insert hook into next chain, yarn over hook, draw through one loop (3 loops on hook), yarn over hook, and draw through 2 loops (2 loops on hook), yarn over hook, and draw through remaining 2 loops on hook (1 loop on hook). This makes one double crochet. Repeat from * to end of chain, turn.
2nd row. Ch2, skip the first double * 1 double in next double, repeat from * to end of row, working last double into second chain of turning chain, turn.
Repeat 2nd row until the work measures the required length. Remember to check the number of stitches you have worked at the end of each row to maintain the shape of your work.
Always draw up the first stitch to its full height. Proper loop formation gives the finished stitch its full and soft appearance. If the top of the stitch is finished off too loosely a ragged effect will be produced.

Turning chains

When working rows (as opposed to rounds), it is necessary to add extra chain stitches at the beginning of each row as a 'fake' stitch to bring you up to the level of stitching for this row. These extra stitches are called turning chains and count as the first stitch of the row to be worked (unless otherwise stated). To compensate for this extra stitch, you must skip the first stitch of the row and work the first actual pattern stitch into the second stitch of the previous row. At the end of each row the last stitch is then worked into the turning chain of the previous row.
These turning chains give a neat, firm edge to your work. The following table is a guide to the number of chains to be worked to give the right depth of the stitch being replaced.
N.B. Some patterns give directions for working the turning chain at the end of the row before turning to start the next row. You may do this if you prefer, but in this publication the turning chain is given at the beginning of each row.

Single crochet	— 1 turning chain
Short or half double	— 2 turning chain
Double crochet	— 3 turning chain
Treble stitch	— 4 turning chain
Double treble stitch	— 5 turning chain

N.B. 'Chain stitches' usually referred to as 'chain.'

▲ *Beginning single crochet along the first chain*

▼ *Double crochet gives a deeper row*

▲ *Bright and useful potholders, each about 5½in square.*

Potholders

You will find it quite easy to make these gay and useful potholders with the two basic stitches given on the opposite page.

Materials required. For each of the potholders shown in the picture you need about 1oz of knitting worsted yarn. A size I (5.50mm.) crochet hook was used, giving a tension of 4sts to 1in. If necessary, change the hook size until you obtain 4sts to 1in square. The finished holder will then measure about 5½in square. The size is easily adapted by adding 4sts for each extra inch required, and working until the holder is square.

Single crochet potholder (on right)
Begin with 21 ch in main color.
1st row. Into 2nd ch from hook work 1 sc, and 1 sc in each ch across (20sc.) Turn.
2nd row. 2 ch * work 1 sc into next sc, rep from * across working last sc into turning ch, turn.
Repeat 2nd row until you have the size you require to form a square. End off.

Edging—With contrasting color, work 1 sc into last st worked before ending off, work 1 sc into next st, working around the holder from left to right instead of right to left: this gives an added ridged effect to the stitch. Work 1 sc in each st along top and base rows, and 2 sc into every 3rd row along side edges.
Loop—At end of last row work 10 ch and join into last dc with a ss to form a loop. End off and press lightly.

Double crochet potholder (on left)
Begin with 23 ch in main color.
1st row. Into 4th ch from hook. work 1 dc, and 1 dc into each ch across (22 dc). Turn.
2nd row. 3 ch, * work dc in next dc of preceding row, rep from * across, working last dc into turning ch. Turn.
Rep 2nd row until you have the size required to produce a square. End off.
With contrasting yarn work edging and loop as given for single crochet potholder.

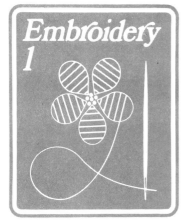

Painting with silks and cottons

Embroidery is at last being recognized as an art form and is finding its way into the museums of modern art. If you are bent on adding decorative touches to your wardrobe and home, or want to design a beautiful panel, it's worth looking through the Creative Hands collection of stitches and designs, both modern and historical, to find inspiration and clear instructions on how to work the stitches.

Nowadays you can create exciting textures and three dimensional effects by using strong designs and color schemes and a fascinating variety of stitches and yarns. But remember, if you are embroidering things which need to be laundered, make sure that all the materials have fast dyes and are washable, and avoid using stitches which are too long, or they may catch and spoil the look of the article.

Designs

Ready-made embroidery designs are usually sold in three ways:
(a) as transfers ready to iron onto your own choice of fabric
(b) already printed on cloth, often in a kit complete with yarns
(c) with charts for counted thread work (for example, cross-stitch).
In later chapters you will discover how to make your own designs, and how to enlarge and adapt.

This gay Czechoslovakian peasant design is worked in simple cross-stitch

Which fabric to work on

You can work embroidery on almost any fabric unless you are following a charted design for counted thread embroidery or drawn-thread work. For both these you need an even-weave cloth. This fabric has an even number of vertical and horizontal threads per square inch, and comes in a variety of colors. It is the best type to use for a beginner, as it helps to keep stitches even.

Well-stocked needlework shops and departments may have even-weave fabrics. You will also find that some linens, cottons and rayons in dress and upholstery fabric departments are also evenly woven, and are equally suitable.

Hoops and frames

Although some embroidery can be worked in the hand, it is usually better for the background fabric to be stretched on either an embroidery hoop or frame. The frame is like a wooden picture frame over which the work is stretched: this will be dealt with in a later chapter. There are four types of embroidery hoop all basically used in the same way. The simplest is the hand-held hoop—a wooden (not a metal) one with a thumbscrew is recommended. The other types are the hoop which clamps onto a table, the hoop on a stand for table or lap, and the hoop on a floor stand.

Setting up a hoop

Adjust the screw so that the rings fit together well. Separate the two rings and place the fabric over the inside ring, centering the design. Press the outside ring over the inside ring until one is inside the other. Gently ease the fabric down until it is taut and smooth, being careful not to pull the fabric on the bias. Tighten the screw if necessary and you are ready to begin. It is important to remove the hoop each time the work is put away.

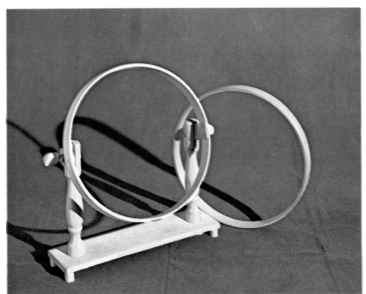

▲ *A table hoop, on its stand, with the outer ring displayed*
▼ *A large hoop can be clamped onto a table, or the arm of a chair*

Yarns and threads

Some techniques require a particular thread or yarn, but in many stitches you can experiment with several kinds.

Yarn/description/uses

1. Brilliant embroidery thread/twisted shiny cotton/ cut work, drawn fabric, drawn-thread work

2. Soft embroidery cotton/ twisted, matt cotton/basic stitches, couching, Hardanger, pattern darning

3. Coton à broder/twisted, shiny cotton/basic stitches, cut work, drawn-thread work, Hardanger, Holbein, smocking, Whitework

4. Crewel wool/twisted, matt wool strands, separable/basic crewel embroidery stitches, couching, needlepoint

5. Slub cotton/knitting cotton uneven surface/couching

6. Tapestry wool/twisted, matt wool/basic stitches, couching, pattern darning, needlepoint

7. Six-strand embroidery floss/twisted separable shiny/ basic stitches, counted thread work, drawn fabric and drawn-thread work.

8. Pearl cotton/twisted, shiny cotton, No.3 thick, No.5 medium, No.8 thin/ basic stitches, Blackwork, counted thread work, drawn fabric and drawn-thread work, Hardanger, smocking

9. Mohair/fluffy knitting yarn/ basic stitches (limited use), couching

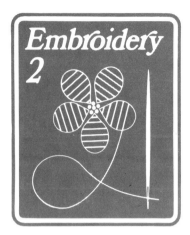

Stitch families and pattern darning

Stitches are divided into families, or groups, and the main families are line, flat, looped, chained, knotted, filling, composite and couching.

The stitch guide begins with simple running stitch and shows you some decorative effects you can achieve by using pattern darning. If you want to try them out immediately, see if you have a plain bath towel in the linen closet. You will notice that there is a 'flat' border between the main area of terrycloth and the towel edge which can be pattern darned in colors to match the bathroom scheme. Always try to practice new stitches on a scrap of cloth or an old garment before embarking on your best linen. Only by experimenting will you discover just which stitch and color combinations are the most successful together.

Remember, whenever you begin to embroider, start by making a knot in the thread, anchor the knot with a few stitches and then continue to embroider. When you have finished, just snip the knot off close to the material so that the thread is perfectly flat and secure.

Running stitch

This stitch is worked horizontally from right to left. Pass the needle over and under the fabric, making the upper stitches the same length and the under ones half as long (also keeping them the same length as each other). For example over 6 threads, under 3, over 6.

Finishing off

To finish off, work one or two back stitches into the reverse side of the work so that they do not show through on the right side.
N.B. When you are doing embroidery, never pull your thread too tight or it will pucker the fabric.
This Bulgarian border shows how even the humble running stitch can be built up into rich motifs with pattern darning. You will

Simple running stitch can make this rich Bulgarian border

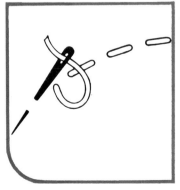

find the same sort of pattern-darned designs on peasant skirts, tote-bags and rugs in Greece, often in corn yellow, red and white on black cloth; or red, black, white and yellow on blue.

Pattern darning

This is an easy and quick method of decorating cloth with simple running stitch, and makes beautiful borders for household linen, children's dresses, and any other garment which needs livening up. Running stitches of varying lengths can be worked in rows to build up into a regular pattern. This is often known as huck embroidery as it was usually worked on huck, a cloth especially used for hand towels. You can also put a running stitch border on a terry towel by working the pattern on the flat surface of the material, near the ends of the towel, not on the raised pile itself. Remember, too, that towels need heavy and frequent washing, so use washable threads.

Fabrics. Suitable fabrics for pattern darning are any even-weave materials like linen and wool. Simply weave or darn the thread into the ground fabric, keeping the tension even.

Threads. Use six-strand floss or pearl cotton for linen or cotton towels, tablecloths and napkins and use tapestry wool for woolen fabrics. Pattern darning can also be done on knitted garments or very loose tweeds using narrow velvet ribbon.

Brick Pattern

1st row. Under 13 threads, over 3 threads, under 2, over 3, under 2, over 3, under 13. Repeat right along border, and do as many rows as required to form the block of stitches.
2nd row. Over 3, under 2, over 3, under 2, over 3, under 13. Repeat as often as needed.

Diabolo pattern

(o=over   u=under)
1st row. o12 u6. *2nd row.* o10 u8. *3rd row.* o8 u10. *4th row.* o6 u12. *5th row.* o4 u14. *6th row.* o2 u16. *7th row.* o2 u16. *8th row.* o4 u14. *9th row.* o6 u12. *10th row.* o8 u10. *11th row.* o10 u8. *12th row.* o12 u6.

Serpentine pattern

(o=over   u=under)
1st row. Across: o2 u2 o2 u2 o2 u2 o2. Up: u2 o2 o2 u2 o2 u2.
Across: o2 u2 o2 u2 o2 u2 o2 u2 o2 u2.
Down: o2 u2 o2 u2 o2 u2. Across: begin again.
2nd row. Same as first, but start with two stitches under, and work on alternate stitches.

Plaid pattern

Using regular running stitch (in this case over 3 and under 3), work five lines of color across the material to form a stripe. Repeat these stripes at regular intervals, and then repeat the whole process with vertical stripes in the same or a different set of colors. You can work out different patterns by varying the number of lines and the color of the stripes, or you can do it diagonally to give a crisscross effect.

Hexagram pattern

This pattern is ideal for livening plain dresses or table linen. The effect is achieved by the use of running stitches on different levels. Follow the picture carefully in four different colors, or four tones of the same color.

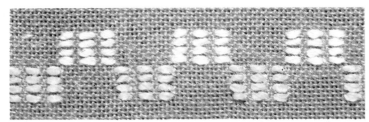

Brick patterns are easily formed by regularly spaced stitches

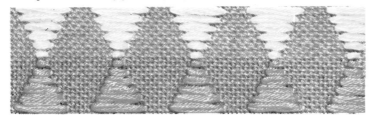

Vary the length of your stitches for a solid Diabolo effect

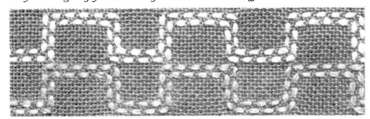

The Serpentine pattern gives a light, fluid design

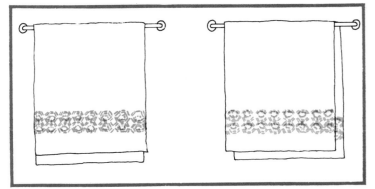

▲ *Pattern darned towels.* ▼ *Hexagram pattern, for a '3-D' effect*

▲ *Gay plaid pattern, above, is useful for a decorative all-over effect*

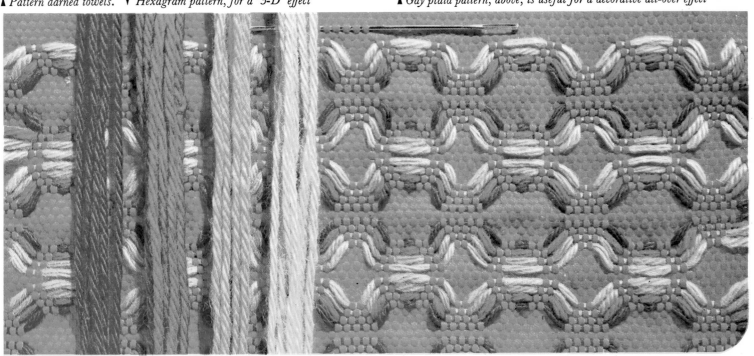

From cuff-links to carpets

Needle-point 1

From the time that someone called the famous Bayeux panel a tapestry, people have been confused about what is embroidery, what is tapestry and what is needlepoint.

In fact, the Bayeux panel is an example of early English embroidery, worked in wools on a linen fabric. Tapestry is always woven, in patterns and pictures, on a loom, with small sections woven individually, then stitched together by hand. The next time you visit a museum, look carefully at the tapestries and you'll see how small some sections are.

Needlepoint is embroidery on canvas. It was very popular in England and Europe from the early sixteenth century until the mid-eighteenth century, but then it marked time, until it was recently revived, Now traditional needlepoint stitches are being used in fabulous modern designs, often with a wide variety of unusual new yarns.

Colorful, textured and tough

The attraction of needlepoint today, apart from the fact that it is handmade and not mass produced, is that all-over embroidery on canvas makes objects and decorations which are really tough and hard-wearing.

It is simple to do, and you have only to visit the yarn counter of any shop to be inspired. Brilliant wools, metallic threads, stranded shiny cottons, soft matt cottons, new nubbly-textured wools and bright plastic raffia all come in a myriad of beautiful colors.

As well as the color, the success of all needlepoint depends upon the texture of the stitches and the threads.

Know your needlepoint

Type of needlepoint	Stitches per inch
Petit point	20 or more
Needlepoint	14 to 18
Gros point	8 to 12
Quick point (or large gros point)	3½ to 7

Canvas size

The canvas must be firm, supple, and evenly woven, and the number of threads to an inch can vary from 24 per inch for fine work, to 3½ per inch for very coarse work.

There are two types, single thread canvas and double thread canvas. You can also use evenly woven fabrics such as Aida cloth, or Hardanger, and even-weave linens or woolen fabrics.

Single thread canvas is measured by the number of threads to the inch and double thread canvas is measured by the number of double threads to the inch. Single weave canvas is the best to use since it is possible to embroider a wide variety of stitches on it, whereas double weave is restricted to four or five only.

Needles

Use tapestry needles with large eyes and blunt points. They are available in a variety of sizes, of which sizes 18-22 are the most popular, but size 14 is better for very coarse material.

Frames

Needlepoint should be worked in a frame. This helps you to maintain the correct shape of the work while it is being embroidered. Small items which you can easily hold in your hand need not be framed.

Floral design, typical of nineteenth-century needlepoint, with soft muted colors, careful shading, and an ornate over-all appearance. Threads of canvas have been separated to produce petit point for fine, delicate stitches.

Yarns

In needlepoint the stitches must completely cover the canvas. Yarns are available in differing thicknesses and some are made up of several individual strands which are twisted together but can be separated as required. To cover the canvas you need to use the correct thickness of yarn. If, however, the yarn coverage looks thin, you should pad it out with the technique known as tramming to fill the space. Never use too long a yarn, as it will wear thin and your work will look uneven and tired. If you find the yarn becoming thin or fluffy, start a new length of yarn at once. It is usually quicker to use a short length—which is a yarn about 12 to 14 inches long.

A modern cushion designed by Joan Nicholson, with abstract pattern repeats, and clear bright colors which blend well together

The right yarn for the canvas

1. Double thread canvas (6 through 15 available)
12 double threads to 1in shown.
Yarns: tapestry yarn, crewel yarn, 4-ply knitting yarns, pearl cotton, 6-strand floss, metallic yarns, stranded pure silk.
2. Double thread canvas (7 through 15 available)
10 double threads to 1in shown.
Yarns as for No. 1 plus knitting worsted, plastic raffia.
3. Petit point canvas (18 and 24 available)
20 threads to 1in shown.
Yarns as for No.1.
4. Single weave canvas (10, 12, 14, 16, 18 available)
18 threads to 1in shown.
Yarns as for No.1 and No.2 plus knitting yarns in a variety of textures such as mohair, tweed, metallic and wool mixtures, soft embroidery cotton, carpet thrums, rug yarn, applied braids and cords, spinning yarns.
5. Single weave (10, 12, 14, 16, 18 available)
12 threads to 1in shown.
Yarns as for No.1 and No.2 and No.4, using more than one thickness of yarn where necessary, plus fine ribbons, strings.

Check off your canvas information against the picture on the right ▶

Collector's Piece

The Bradford Carpet

This fine carpet, dated about 1600, was formerly the property of the Earl of Bradford at Castle Bromwich in England. The complete carpet measures sixteen feet long by six feet wide and was at one time used to adorn a table. It is now displayed under glass in the Victoria and Albert Museum in London, where it covers a complete wall. The carpet was designed to an exact size so that the lattice work center just covered the table top, with equal edges hanging all around. Because the entire design is worked in fine tent stitch (petit point), the canvas has been distorted from its rectangular shape into a parallelogram. It is therefore 13 inches out of square along a short edge and consequently the figures in the illustration are leaning. Some areas which are left unfinished show the canvas to be linen, with about twenty threads to the inch. The stitching is extremely even and of a delicate coloring. This carpet is a typical example of the Elizabethan tradition, when silk thread was used throughout, giving a soft sheen to the surface.

The design is simple and realistic, as this small section of the border illustrates. The undulating landscape continues entirely around the perimeter of the carpet giving a charming impression of rural life in the 17th century. Against a picturesque background of cottages and flowering trees, the people of the village go busily about their activities. Closer examination of this section reveals a series of scenes portraying hunting, shooting and fishing.

One stitch and a batch of buttons

Needle-point 2

With just one basic needlepoint stitch you can make your own buttons in dozens of different yarns and motifs. A needlepoint vest would look stunning with its own buttons worked to match; they could also be fun on a coat or suit, or even worn on their own as unusual earrings. This page gives you the instructions for making the buttons, plus three button designs (shown on the right) using half cross-stitch, with or without tramming.

How to make the buttons

Use do-it-yourself buttons which come in many sizes from most notions departments. Here are three designs to start with, plus a chart to show you the right fabric and thread to use for each size of button. Always use either a very fine canvas, Aida cloth (which is softer than canvas), or an even-weave cloth.

The chart gives the turning allowance which will take the worked material safely over the edge to the back of the button. Simply draw a circle around the button, allowing enough for the turnings as well, and you are ready to start, but do not cut out until the needlepoint is finished.

N.B. The buttons are simple to assemble and come with easy-to-follow instructions on the package. Use half cross-stitch, trammed, or untrammed, as you find it necessary. Follow the exact number of stitches shown in the picture. To work out your own patterns, plot them out first on squared graph paper with colored pencils.

Trim button size + turning	Fabric threads to the inch	Suggested threads
$\frac{3}{4}$in + $\frac{1}{8}$in turning	28	3 strands of 6-strand floss 2 strands of crewel wool pearl cotton
$\frac{7}{8}$in + $\frac{1}{8}$in turning	25	4 strands of 6-strand floss
$1\frac{1}{8}$in + $\frac{1}{4}$in turning	18	6 strands of 6-strand floss
$1\frac{1}{2}$in + $\frac{1}{4}$in turning	14 Aida cloth (14 blocks of thread to the inch)	6 strands of 6-strand floss tapestry wool raffia 4-ply knitting

How to start

1. Find the center of the piece of canvas by folding it in half twice; mark the center lightly with a colored crayon or thread. Start in the center, but instead of using a knot, draw the needle up through the canvas, leaving a tail about half-an-inch long at the back.

2. Hold this yarn close to the canvas and work over it, binding it in with the first few stitches (which are seen here from the back).

To finish off

Darn the yarn into the stitches at the back of your work to secure it. To continue with a new yarn, darn its tail into back of the previous row.
Never allow any of these yarns to accumulate in one place as this results in unsightly bumps.

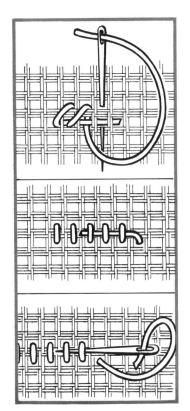

Half cross-stitch

Half cross-stitch is hard-wearing—smooth, flat and ideal for things which need to be tough, like stool and chair seats. But because it is so simple to do, it is one of the best stitches to use for any small scale patterns.
This stitch is worked as shown, from left to right. Up through the canvas from bottom left, down through the next 'hole' on top right. This makes a diagonal stitch on the front and a short straight stitch on the back.
Fasten off at end of each patch of color and begin again so that you do not carry long lengths of thread at the back.

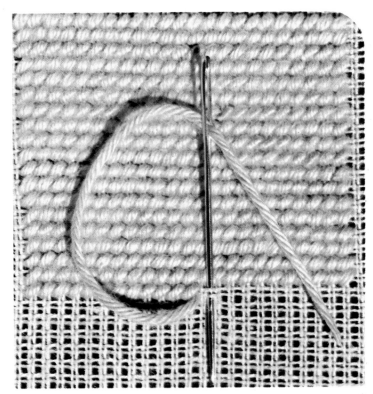

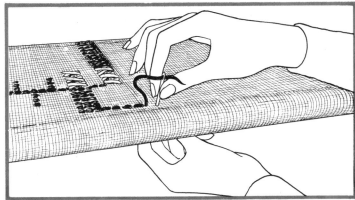

Top *Half cross-stitch.* Center *The drawing shows the method used when working in a frame.* Bottom *The stitch worked over tramming*

Tramming

Tramming is a padding stitch which is used when the yarn is not thick enough to cover the canvas completely.
The tramming yarn runs along each horizontal single canvas thread, or pair of threads (called 'tramlines') as shown in the illustration at the right. Bring the yarn up through these tramlines, leaving a short tail at the back. Work in overlapping tramming stitches, not more than five inches long, for the length of your working area. Then take the yarn down through the tramlines again. Work the stitch over the tramming yarn, binding in the tramming tails as you go.

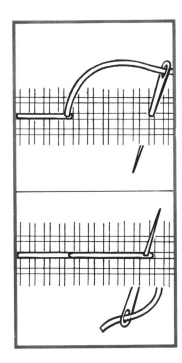

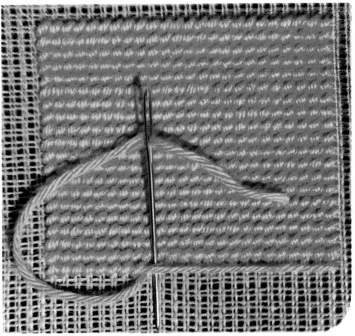

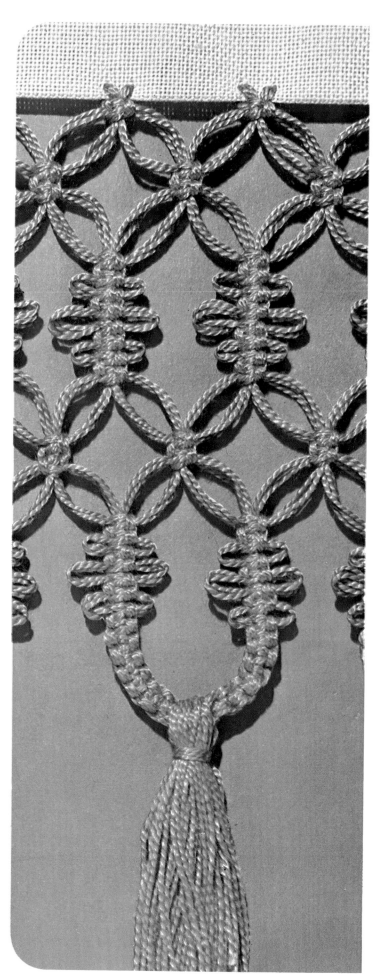

Rediscovering The Gentle Arts

If you've ever admired a delicate piece of handmade lace, a display of fragile embroidery on net, or a flamboyantly fringed shawl in the Paris collections, then you should find the Gentle Arts chapters fascinating.

Once these delicate crafts were the pursuit of ladies of leisure. Today designers, teachers and art students are making bold macramé screens and fringes out of bright rug wools and thick string; they are using daisymaker frames for a modern version of 'Teneriffe Lace', and working bobbin lace on giant bobbins with metallic yarns for glittering, brilliant, three-dimensional effects.

These Gentle Arts chapters give the basic techniques, and many facts to use for more advanced work. They cover both the traditional craft techniques and also introduce thoroughly up-to-date ideas for translating them into modern designs.

1. Macramé. Tools: hands.
Macramé is a knotting and fringing technique and, depending on the thread or string used, you can make anything from a tough string beach bag to a magnificent silky fringe for an evening stole.

2. Needle-made lace. Tools: needle.
This came originally from the Italian Alps. It is made with a needle and is crisp, geometric, hard-wearing lace, ideal as an insertion or edging for blouses and household linen. (It looks particularly charming as a trim for linen table mats.)

3. Tatting. Tools: shuttle, crochet hook.
Tatting is so easy to do and carry around to fill in any odd moments that the French call it 'frivolité'. 19th-century women decorated their clothes with tatting in brightly colored silks, but today it trims hankies, collars, tablecloths and mats.

4. Embroidery on net. Tools: needle.
Mediterranean girls knot their own net for filet lace, but you can take a short cut and buy net and embroider it. In later issues you will find ideas for beautiful curtains, bedspreads and table linen.

5. Teneriffe Lace. Tools: pins, needle, daisymaker.
These lacy webs originated in Brazil where they were joined together to make lavish mantillas. Today they can be used to make just one flower motif to decorate a child's pinafore pocket, or to make a whole garden-full for a cushion cover.

6. Bobbin Lace. Tools: pins, bobbins, pillow.
The art of bobbin lace has not changed since its early days as a cottage industry in Italy and France. The lace is exquisite and makes lovely edgings and table centers, which are a real compensation for all the careful work it involves.

◄ *Exotic-looking macramé edging, with deep silky fringes*

▲ *Crisply geometric needle-made lace (2.) for an elegant, strong insertion*
▼ *A traditional flowing edging made from bobbin lace (6.)*

▲ *Tatting, (3.) the Victorian favorite, makes a gently romantic motif*
▼ *A light texture, for a rich design, using embroidery on net (4.)*

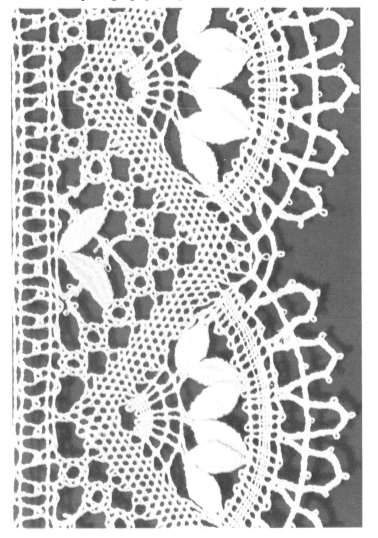

Fringe benefit

Fringes are really very easy to make. There is no sewing involved, just simple knotting worked directly onto a finished edge. Start with something simple like a scarf or a lampshade. Then, when you feel more confident, you can adapt the patterns to decorate cushions, curtains, bedspreads, blinds and clothes, making them look just as luxurious as the custom-made ones which are so terribly expensive.

Suitable yarns for fringing
You can make fringes out of any yarn you choose, and work them onto practically any fabric. Just be sure to suit the thickness of the yarn to the weight of the fabric you are using. You can use wool, silk or cotton, but it is wise to choose a firmly twisted yarn so that it won't unravel.

Other materials you will need:
☐ Firm padded cushion. If you are fringing a soft edge such as on a tablecloth or curtains, it is helpful to anchor the work on a heavy padded cushion or rolled-up towel while you knot the fringe. Simply pin the fabric to it along the hem line, so that the knotting threads can hang loose. A lot of fringing can be worked directly onto articles with rigid edges, such as lampshades and window shades.
☐ Crochet hook or needle. To produce a neat edging you can use either to thread the lengths of yarn onto the fabric. A crochet hook can be used with loosely woven fabrics, while a needle is more suitable for closely woven materials—a chenille needle or short darning needle is best, as it has a large eye but is sharp enough to pierce the fabric.
☐ A metal comb. You will find this useful for straightening out the threads.
☐ A pair of scissors
☐ Pins

Length of yarn for fringing
As a general rule, you should cut the yarn in pieces three times the length of the pattern you want, plus twice the tassel length required (i.e. for a finished fringe with a 6in pattern and a 3in tassel, the yarn should be cut in 24in lengths: 3 x 6in pattern, plus 2 x 3in tassel). However, some fringe patterns take up different amounts of yarn, depending on their thickness, so it is advisable always to work a simple section of the pattern before starting the final fringe, to be sure your calculations are correct.

Threading on the yarn
Prepare the yarn in bunches and pull each bunch through the edge of the fabric from front to back, leaving equal lengths on each side. If you are using fine yarns, you can thread three or four threads at a time. With thicker yarns, however, you may find it easier to thread one length at a time.

Make the bunches as thick as you like, but remember, the thicker they are, the bolder and more dramatic the effect will be.

To prevent the threads from becoming tangled when working long fringes or while threading, tie each bunch in a firm, but temporary, slip knot, as shown in the illustration.

The simple knot
When you have threaded the bunches evenly through the fabric, secure each of them with a simple knot (or half hitch) near the edge of the fabric. Always tie the knots in the same direction. Tie the knot loosely at first, then maneuver it into place with a pin or the blunt end of a needle, as shown, before tightening up.

Alternating simple knot fringe
This is an easy way to fringe a lampshade or scarf. Cut the yarn into the required lengths, thread the bunches through the fabric (with the lampshade, take them over the frame as well) at ½in intervals, and work a row of simple knots, as described. Now work two rows of alternating simple knots — tying half the threads from one bunch to half of the next — to give a lattice effect. The remaining yarn forms the tassels. Always use a pin to coax the knots into the correct position, or they will look uneven and spoil the finished effect.

Lampshade and scarf decorated with alternating simple knot fringe

Alternating simple knot fringe with variation
Cut the yarn into the required lengths, thread the bunches through the fabric at ½in intervals, as before, and work 5 rows in alternating simple knots. Work the 6th row in simple knots (not alternating) directly below the 5th row, to form columns of yarn. Now work 4 more rows of alternating simple knots and leave the remaining yarn to form tassels hanging below.

You can vary the length of this fringe to suit whatever article you are working it on. Make it short to trim a bedspread or curtains, or long to transform a shawl.

There will be instructions for more fringes in the following fringing chapters, so practice with this simple method now so that you become familiar with knotting and spacing the knots correctly.

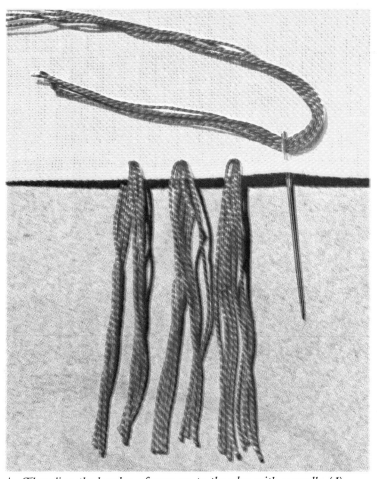

▲ *Threading the bunches of yarn on to the edge with a needle (1)*
▼ *To avoid tangles, tie long bunches with a slip knot before starting (2)*

▲ *Three steps in tying the simple knot (3)*
▼ *Alternating simple knot fringe which gives a lattice effect (4)*

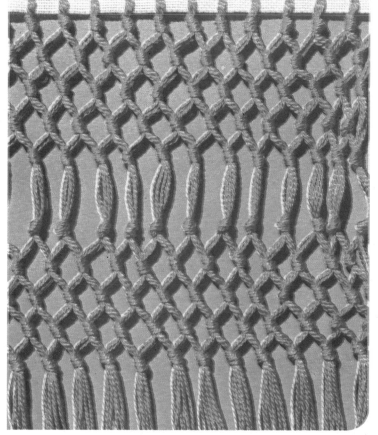

The secret of successful dressmaking

Dressmaking is creative and satisfying, just so long as the finished garment turns out the way you want it! Choosing a fabric and the style which suits you best is great fun, but making it fit you well is really the secret of achieving that individual, figure-flattering couture look.
N.B. Remember when reading Creative Hands that "sewing" refers to hand sewing, and "stitching" refers to machine work.

Dressmaking the Creative Hands way

Creative Hands shows you how to make clothes which really do fit. It's a course, a complete reference book to basic dressmaking knowledge, a library of designs for adults and children, and most rewarding of all, it shows you how to be your own designer.

Starting to sew—or in need of a refresher course?

Each step-by-step chapter is simple and easy to follow because every technique you need is either clearly illustrated or fully explained. The whole course is straightforward. It gets you sewing successful garments right from the start, and it also gives sound advice on how to choose important equipment—like a sewing machine—and how to get the best use out of it.
But what makes this course so exceptional is the special Dressmaker's Pattern Pack which we have designed for you to use with the Creative Hands instructions. The Pack has two purposes. First, it provides a range of garments for you to make which incorporate basic dressmaking techniques. Second, it provides clear, recognizable pattern shapes which are easy to use when it comes to the more creative side of pattern adapting.

If you are an experienced dressmaker

This isn't an ordinary home dressmaking manual—it's full of the tricks-of-the-trade secrets which most professional dressmakers never give away. What's more, it fully explains the reasons for using certain techniques and finishes so you can not only extend your dressmaking knowledge, but also get perfect results.
Moreover, the aspect you'll probably find most interesting is pattern adapting and style conversion. The chapters on using the Dressmaker's Pattern Pack show methods of designing with pattern shapes to give you unlimited scope. Add to this the ideas from the Fashion Flair pages and you have what it takes to design your own clothes with supple ease, perfect fit and integrated detail.

Sewing for children

Many of the chapters are devoted to inexpensive sewing for children of all ages. The Creative Hands patterns are simple, attractive and adaptable in the same way as the adult designs.

Have you got a figure problem?

Creative Hands sympathizes with you and sets out to help you solve it. There are special sections on the importance of selecting the right fabric and design to flatter your figure type and on fitting, especially for the larger sizes. It's good news, too, that commercial paper pattern houses are giving more thought to designing flattering, fashion-conscious clothes for the fuller figure.

Talking about commercial paper patterns

All the techniques in the following chapters apply equally well to dressmaking with commercial paper patterns. Creative Hands sets out to influence you in one direction only—to help you make clothes more successfully with a look that's all your own.

The Dressmaker's Pattern Pack

The key to dressmaking the Creative Hands way is the Dressmaker's Pattern Pack, given in Volume 22. It is a set of basic graph patterns for a blouse, a dress and cuffs. Instructions on how to make your graph patterns are given on page 78. The patterns are straightforward, easy to use and, more important, they are adaptable. This is the key to being your own designer.

Designing with the Pattern Pack

Creative Hands first takes you through the important stages of achieving a perfect fit—making a muslin pattern, fitting and transferring fitting corrections to the basic pattern—then, using your personalized pattern shapes, step-by-step into the exciting realms of designing. You can create an entire wardrobe of clothes with the Pattern Pack. These pages illustrate just a few of the variations, but, inspired by exciting new fabrics and with Creative Hands helping to develop your skills, you'll discover the variations are endless.

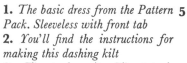

3

4

8

1. *The basic dress from the Pattern Pack. Sleeveless with front tab*
2. *You'll find the instructions for making this dashing kilt*
3. *The tunic suit. The top is adapted from the basic dress pattern*
4. *Variation on the basic blouse. The dirndl is a skirt adaptation*
5. *These gay little dresses are adapted from a basic graph pattern*
6. *The Pattern Pack basic pants. The lines are straight and slimming*
7. *Vest and culottes. From a special Creative Hands pattern*
8. *Basic dress adapted for evening*

5

6

7

The Basic Tools for Successful Sewing

Any sewing aid which is specially designed to make your work easier is a good idea. But now that the home dressmaking industry offers you so many gadgets, it's difficult to decide which is really necessary. Here is a list of basic aids which you will need for the simplest dressmaking, and which will help you to achieve more professional results.

Basic equipment

Sewing machine. The most important piece of equipment in the sewing room is, of course, the sewing machine. Whether it is a treasured family heirloom or a gleaming new model, it is very important that the machine stands on a firm base at a comfortable working height, and that a light shines directly on the needle when stitching.

Hand sewing needles. Size 8 for dressmaking. Size 9 for sewing fir fabrics such as silks or chiffons. Size 7 for heavier work such as sewing on buttons. Use either the medium length sharps or long millinery needles, whichever suits you best.

Pins. Steel dressmaking pins, at least 1 inch or $1\frac{3}{16}$ inch long, are the best. Nickel-plated pins may bend during use and could damage fine cloth. Glasshead pins are very sharp (made from needle rejects), but have limited use since the heads break easily.

Scissors. You'll need a good pair of sharp cutting shears, with handles that comfortably fit the hand (left-handed shears are available for those who need them), also a pair of small dressmaking scissors to use while making up your garments.

Tailor's chalk. At least two pieces are essential for marking, one white, one blue.

Tape measure. A good tape measure shouldn't stretch, so use one made of glass fiber.

Tracing wheel. This is used for marking pattern outlines on to fabric. Choose one made from steel with sharp points.

Dressmaker's tracing paper. A special type of carbon paper for use with a sharp-pointed tracing wheel. Use with care, if at all, as it can mark delicate fabrics. Tailor's chalk is preferable.

Thimble. A steel-lined thimble is best since it gives longer wear. It should fit the middle finger of your sewing hand.

Triangle. This is also known as a tailor's square and is used to obtain fabric grain lines in pattern making.

Yardstick. This is used for measuring hems and connecting points for straight seams. It should be firm and straight.

Steam iron. A medium-weight iron with heat controls is essential. Use cleaning fluid to keep the base of the iron clean.

Ironing board. This should stand firmly and have a smooth-fitting cover securely attached under the board. Covers made of heavily dressed cloth are not suitable, since the dressing can be transferred to the iron, particularly when wet.

Press cloth. A two foot square piece of finely woven cotton or lawn is essential for steam pressing. Thicker cloths hold too much moisture and may harm the fabric. A good press cloth should be free from imperfections such as holes, frayed edges and prominent grains, all of which can easily be transferred to the fabric being pressed. Also, it shouldn't contain any dressing because this will stick to the iron and mark the fabric.

Press board. This is necessary for pressing pleats and flat surfaces. You can make one quite simply from a square of cork or plywood about 30 inches by 20 inches. Pad it with a folded blanket and cover with sheeting.

Buying a new sewing machine?

A sewing machine is a big investment so if you're thinking of making a purchase, it is important to know the types which are available and what they will do.

There are many makes of sewing machines on the market, all differently priced, but today's machines fit into three main categories: straight-stitch, swing-needle (or zigzag) and swing-needle automatic. Here are some tips on what to expect from each type of machine.

Straight-stitch. This machine sews only with a straight stitch and most will sew in reverse as well as forward. Some attachments come with the machine and others can be obtained at extra cost. Ask about this when buying. Straight-stitch machines are in the lowest price bracket and prices vary according to quality.

Swing-needle. This machine does zigzag stitching in addition to straight stitching. The zigzag stitch is useful for finishing seams, hems, making lace insertions and buttonholes. Some swing-needle machines have an automatic buttonhole reverse and most come with a good range of attachments. These machines are in the medium price range.

Swing-needle automatic. This machine has all the facilities of the straight-stitch and swing-needle, but it can also do embroidery. Various effects can be achieved by inserting special discs into the machine or by engaging settings which are built into the mechanism. These are the most expensive machines to buy.

How to choose a machine

If you need a machine for light dressmaking only, any of the previously mentioned types, straight-stitch, swing-needle, or swing-needle automatic, will be suitable.

If you want a general-purpose machine to cope with all the household sewing and mending, be sure that the machine you choose will take heavy work.

If you need a machine for tailoring, it is advisable to choose from the straight-stitch and swing-needle ranges only. A fully automatic swing-needle machine has only a limited use for tailoring.

Testing

In most cases, it is possible to test a machine at home for a few days and this will give you a chance to see if it is really suitable for your needs. If you do have a machine on approval, first of all read the instruction manual carefully to see if there are any restrictions on how you can use the machine.

Here is your opportunity to try the machine on different types of cloth, especially those you are most likely to be working with later on. If you are testing the machine for heavier work, remember to stitch over double seams in a medium-thick cloth. See that the machine passes the work through evenly, that it does not hesitate in front of the seams or jump off when it has stitched through the thickest part.

It is important to test the speed of the machine. For instance, if you think you will be doing a lot of household sewing, particularly items like sheets, bedspreads, and curtains which have long, monotonous seams, then you will want a machine that can cope with this work quickly as well as correctly.

Do not be misled by a claim that a machine will 'break in'. Many machines are set at one speed only, but some of the newest and most expensive have a built-in gear to increase the stitching rate. You can adjust the speed slightly by regulating machine controls, but transmissions vary and some machines will operate faster than others. By learning to operate the controls, you will always be able to use a very fast machine at slow speeds, but if a machine stitches slowly, it is because the transmission is low-geared.

When you're testing, make sure that the pressure foot and tension are at the correct setting. Settings vary with different manufacturers, and these details will be pointed out in the manual. Also check that the stitch size is correct for the setting engaged, and that the thread number and needle size are correct too.

How to find the correct thread number and needle size

Many machines are tested, and set, to work best at a certain thread number. Therefore, find out from the manual which are the recommended numbers for that machine.

To help you, here is a chart setting out the comparisons between the American and Continental sizes.

Thread number	Needle sizes	Continental needle sizes	Type of material
40	16	100	Heavy fabrics
50	14 12	90 80	Medium fabrics
60	10	70	Light-weight fabrics

Stitch size and tension

To obtain the correct stitch size and tension (the tightness balance between both threads) adjust the controls on the machine as shown below.

For the top thread feed control, adjust the dial on the front of the tension spring, which reads from 0-9. The higher the number, the tighter the thread feed.

To adjust the tension on the bobbin, loosen or tighten the tiny screw on top of the bobbin case which holds down a spring in the shape of a little steel clip.

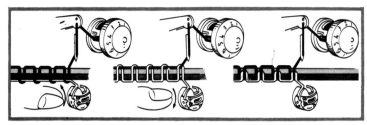

Different gauges of sewing thread, such as silk, cotton and mercerized cotton, can affect stitch size and the tension. So, before making a garment, always test the stitches on layers of the material you are preparing to sew.

Finally, having tested the performance of the machine before buying, satisfy yourself that it carries a good guarantee.

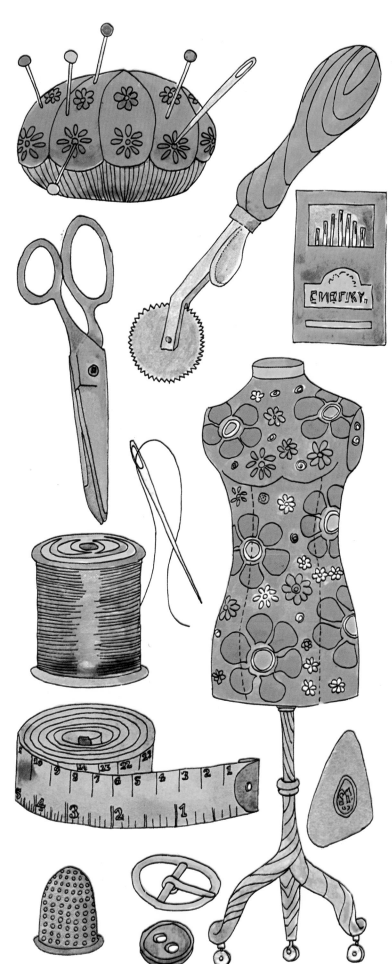

How do you measure up?

The important point to aim for in dressmaking is to achieve a really perfect fit. So it is essential that you know exactly what your personal measurements are before you begin. All commercial paper patterns are made to standard sizes, but even if you are one of those rare people with perfect proportions, or you buy a pattern size which should fit your figure type, you may have to make slight adjustments to it. The chart set out on the facing page contains all the measurements you will need to use when working with paper patterns, plus instructions on where to take them. Before filling it in, enlist the help of a friend or a willing husband, and you'll soon have your personal measurement chart to keep by you for constant references whenever you're dressmaking.

Taking your measurements

Study the first two columns carefully before you start so that you will be familiar with all the measuring points, then take the measurements over a smooth-fitting dress, or slip. You will need to pin a length of ½ inch tape or straight seam binding around your waist before you start. This helps you to obtain exact bodice length measurements. Make sure you do not measure tight but allow the tape to run closely over the body without dropping. Of course, you will be using your non-stretch inch tape! It's a good idea to take measurements more than once for complete accuracy and also to take them towards the end of the day, if you intend to make evening clothes, because body measurements can vary between morning and evening. You could even divide the 'Your Measurements' column into a.m. and p.m.!

Why your pattern is larger than you
When you measure through any paper pattern, you'll find that it is larger than your own measurements. This is because every pattern has tolerance, (or ease) built in, so that the garment cut from that pattern feels easy and comfortable to wear.
The standard allowance for ease is 2 inches for bust, 1 inch for waist and 2 inches for hip measurements, but these amounts vary according to the fit of a garment and the fabric used for making it up. Here are two simple examples. If you use a bulky fabric, the standard allowance for ease must be increased by at least 1 inch to 2 inches to allow the bulk of the fabric to settle around the figure. A loosely fitting style, on the other hand, will have extra ease built into it, and the extra amount required will already have been added to the standard ease in the pattern. If you measure through the Creative Hands blouse pattern, which is a semi-fitted style, you can check this for yourself. You'll be coming across the term tolerance, or ease, frequently in the following chapters, where you'll also discover its importance, particularly during the fitting stages of dressmaking.

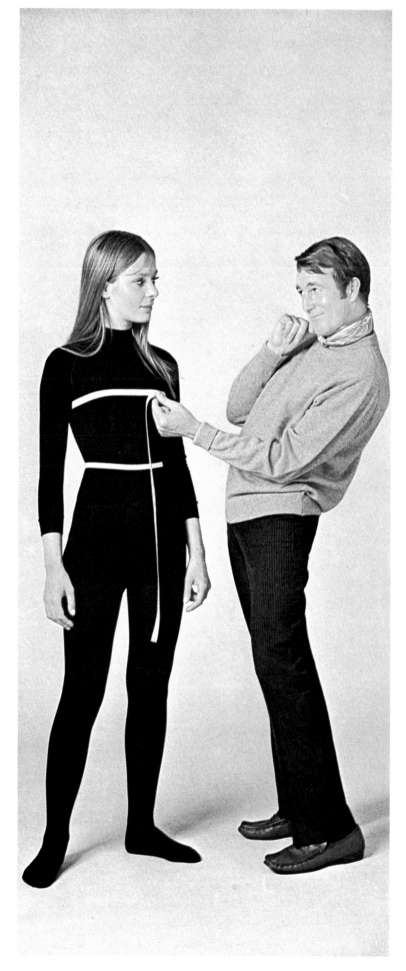

	Where to measure	Your measurements
1. **Bust**	Over fullest part of bust and around back	
2. **Waist**	Lay tape into natural waist curve	
3. **Hips**	Over highest part of seat and thickest part of thighs	
4. **Shoulder**	From neck to imaginary armhole seam	
5. **Shoulder across back**	From armhole seam to armhole seam	
6. **Center back length**	From nape of neck to waist	
7. **Center front length**	From base of neck to waist	
8. **Front length (i)**	From center shoulder to waist	
9. **Front length (ii)**	From center shoulder to highest point of bust	
10. **Width across front**	From armhole seam to armhole seam, half way between shoulder and bustline	
11. **Width across back (i)**	From armhole seam to armhole seam over shoulder blades	
12. **Width across back (ii)**	As 11, with arms extended forward	
13. **Armhole**	Over shoulder point, around underarm, back to shoulder, with arm against body	
14. **Side seam**	From armhole to waist line	
15. **Underarm sleeve seam**	From lowest point of armhole to wrist with arm extended outward 45°	
16. **Outside sleeve length**	From point half way between shoulder and underarm seam, over bent elbow, to wrist	
17. **Sleeve length to elbow**	From shoulder point to elbow	
18. **Neck (i)**	Around base	
19. **Neck (ii)**	Around neck	
20. **Forearm**	Around fullest part of arm muscle	
21. **Wrist**	Over wrist bone	
22. **Top arm**	Around fullest part	
23. **Center back full length**	From nape of neck into waist, to hem	
24. **High hip**	About 3in below waist line over hip bone	
25. **Skirt length**	From waist line over side hip to hem	
26. **Pants depth of crotch**	From center front waist line through crotch to center back waist line	
27. **Pants inside leg**	Stand with legs spread Measure from inside crotch to below ankle bone (Finished length depends on heel height worn.)	

Dressmaking terms

Basting. A continuous row of long, hand or machine, stitches to hold two or more layers of fabric together.

Ease. To hold in fullness without showing gathers or pleats.

Face. To finish raw edges with matching shapes.

Grain. Lengthwise, or warp threads running parallel to the selvage. Crosswise, or weft threads running across fabric from selvage to selvage.

Interfacing. Fabric between facing and garment to support an edge and hold a shape.

Interlining. Inner lining between lining and outer fabric for warmth or bulk.

Marking. Indicating pattern detail on fabric. Showing seam allowance for cutting. Showing fitting corrections.

Nap. Fibrous surface given to cloth in finishing.

Notch. Small 'V' cut in the seam allowance to eliminate bulk in outward-curving seams.

One-way fabrics. Fabrics where the surface interest runs in the same direction. This includes prints, nap or pile as well as warp-knitted fabrics.

Pile. Raised woven-in surface on velvets and fur fabrics.

Slash. To cut along a given line to open a dart or a fold.

Slip-baste. To baste a seam through a folded edge from the outside to match perfectly plaids or stripes for stitching.

Snip. A small cut made either at right angles or at a slant to the raw edge of a seam allowance to enable it to spread and follow a stitched curve.

Stay stitches. A line of stitches made by hand or machine within a seam allowance to prevent stretching.

Tailor's tacks. Tacking stitches made with double thread where every second stitch forms a loop. Can be made in one continuous row or over a few grains of the weave, to form a single tack. Used only to mark pattern detail through two layers of fabric.

Top-stitching. A line of machine stitches made on the outside of a garment parallel to an edge or seam.

Start with a pop-over pinafore

Every little girl needs a pop-over to keep her clothes clean, and if it's got a pretty pocket for her teddy bear or hanky it will be fun to wear. The next four pages include a tracing pattern complete with instructions for hand or machine sewing. Even if you're not very confident about your dressmaking, it's simple to make. Experienced dressmakers will enjoy thinking up other pocket designs based on similar shapes.

▲ *Pop-over seen from the back*
▼ *Pop-over front, with pocket*

Fabric requirements

⅝yd of gingham, 36in wide. ¾yd of contrasting fabric for pocket, or piece 11in by 14in. 3yd of bias binding (for machine finish only). Two buttons. Sewing thread. Embroidery cotton and ½yd of tape (for hand finish only).

Layout and cutting
Fold gingham selvage to selvage and lay out the pattern pieces as shown in the diagrams. Cut ONE pocket in gingham and ONE pocket and handle in contrasting fabric. Mark out seam allowance on all pattern pieces and cut out.

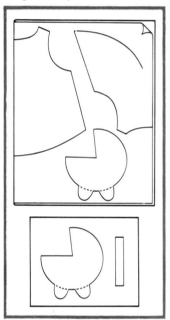

Layout on 36in fabric, with pocket on contrasting piece

Making up
Make line of basting down the center front on fold. Join side seams and shoulder seams. If you work by hand, use backstitch or running stitch. Overcast raw edges.

Running stitch

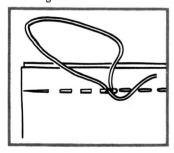

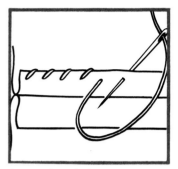

Overcasting stitch

If you work by hand
Turn under, pin and baste seam allowance on neck, armholes and around hem up to the top of center back. Press lightly in position. Work around these edges with alternating blanket stitch. This not only looks attractive but ensures that you catch the folded edge every time.

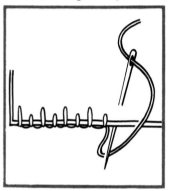

Alternating blanket stitch

Make stitches about $\frac{3}{16}$in apart. On both pocket pieces, turn under seam allowance all around, snipping corners. Wrong sides together, baste pockets together and work same blanket stitch all around.

If you work by machine
Take bias binding, open fold on one side and lay to seam allowance, right sides facing, around neck, armholes and hem. Ease into curves at neck and armholes, pin and stitch together. Turn bias binding to the inside and baste in position. Stitch to pop-over and press, taking care not to stretch edges.
For pocket lay gingham and contrasting fabric pieces together, right sides facing, and stitch around, leaving 2in opening. Snip corners and turn pocket right side out.

Slip stitch opening. Baste around edges and press lightly.

To make loop, by hand and machine
Fold fabric in half lengthwise and stitch. Pull through to outside with the aid of safety pin. Press flat.

To stitch pocket to pop-over and finish
Lay center of pocket on center front of pop-over, with wheels about 1½in from bottom edge. Tuck raw ends of loop for handle under end of baby carriage and stitch pocket, following dash line on pattern. If you stitch by hand, use firm backstitch. Do not sew over blanket stitches.
To fasten pop-over at back, attach two pieces of tape at neck and tie in a bow, or make two loops for buttons on right side of back and attach where shown on pattern. Sew on buttons opposite the loops.

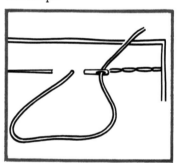

Backstitch

Some pretty ideas for pockets

Of course there's no need to stick to the baby carriage if you have other ideas for pockets, or if you are making more than one pop-over. Use the basic pocket shape—but adapt it in different ways. You can make the shape, minus the wheels, into a boat, and appliqué a white or colored sail to the front of the pop-over. Or, make a basket, with a handle, and then appliqué bright flowers, or richly colored fruits on it.

Pattern for pocket

Solid black line: stitching
line for carriage. Arrows
indicate corners for snipping.
Dash line: for stitching pocket
to pop-over.
Seam allowance to be added:
¼in all around carriage.

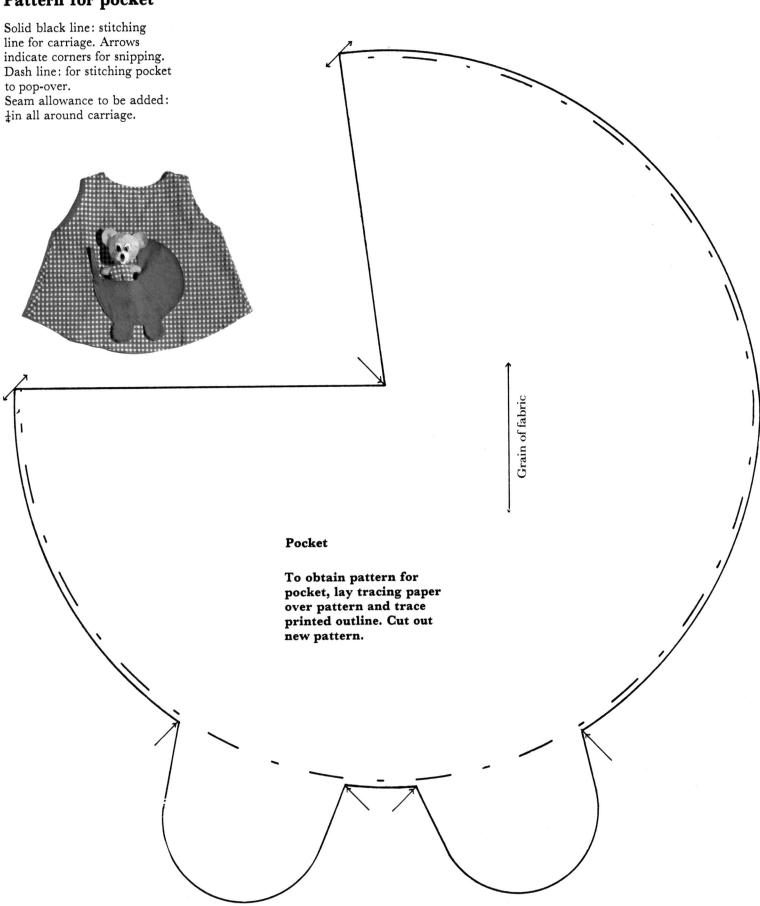

Grain of fabric

Pocket

**To obtain pattern for
pocket, lay tracing paper
over pattern and trace
printed outline. Cut out
new pattern.**

Place on Fold

Grain of fabric

Side Seam

Grain of fabric

Baby carriage handle loop

Grain of fabric

Pattern for front and back of pop-over and baby carriage handle loop

Solid black line: stitching line for front and loop.
Dot and dash line: stitching line for back.
Seam allowance to be added:
$\frac{1}{4}$in to all sides of baby carriage handle loop.
$\frac{1}{2}$in to shoulder and side-seams.
$\frac{1}{4}$in to hem and necklines.

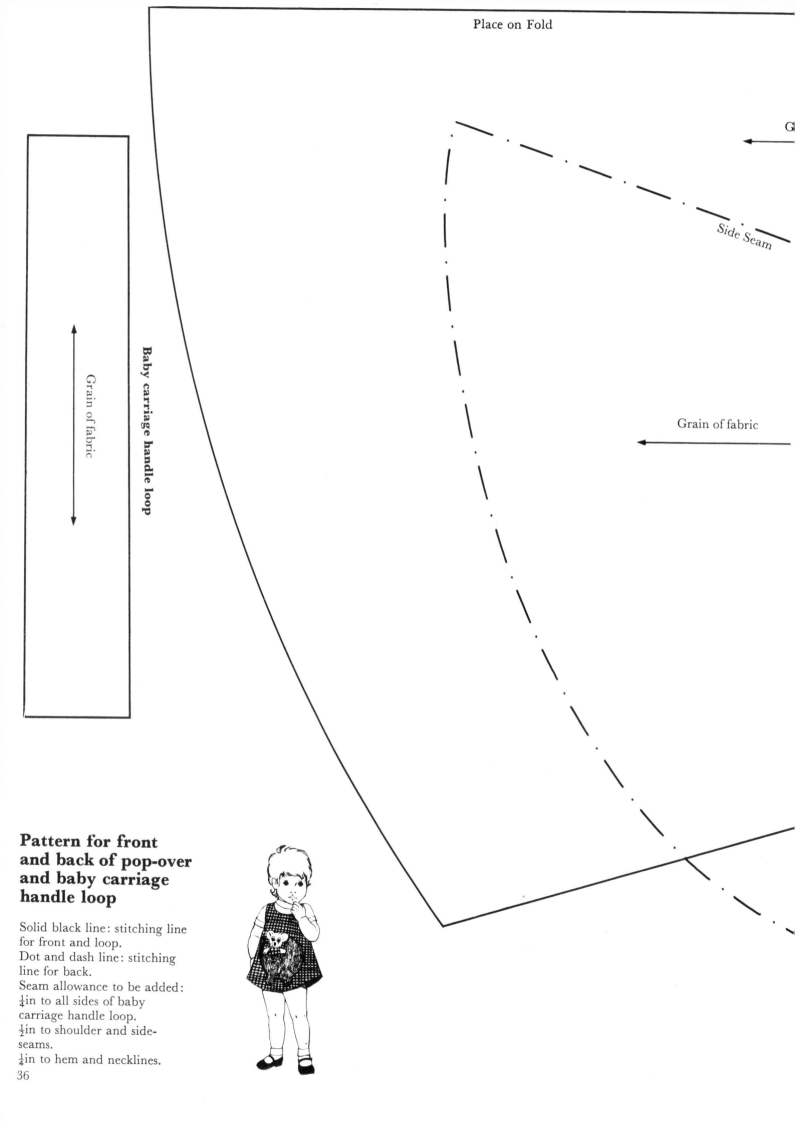

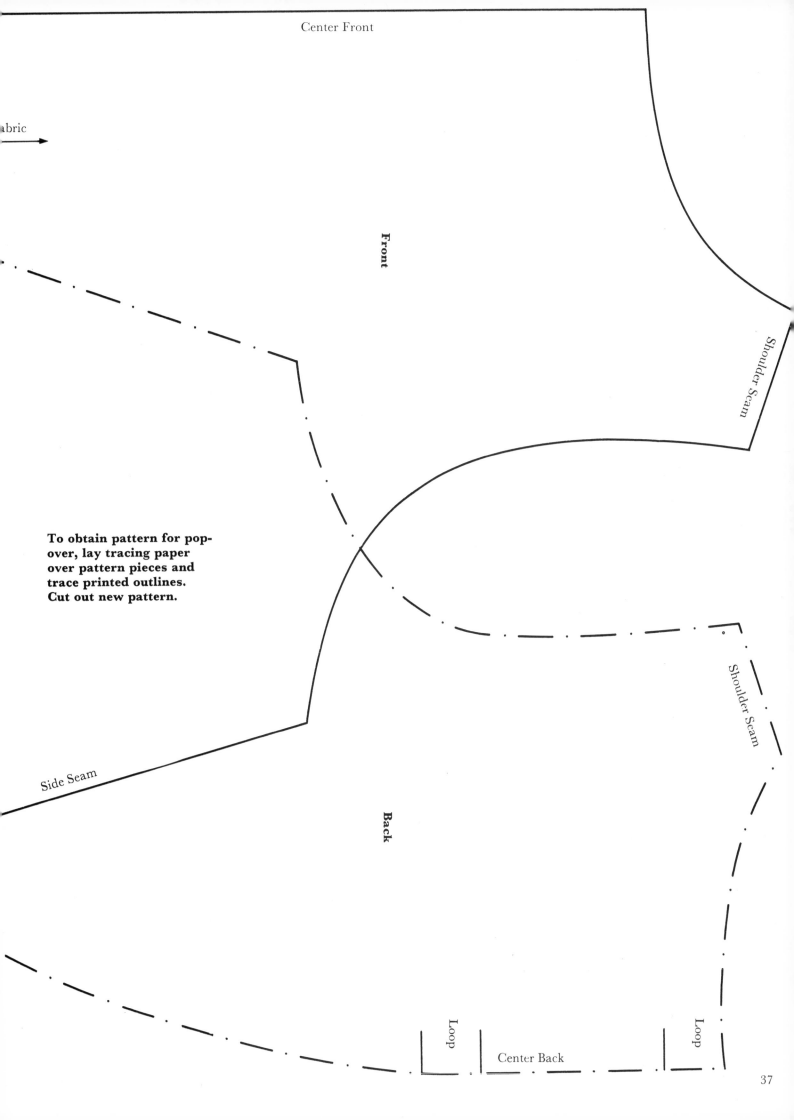

Center Front

Fabric →

Front

Shoulder Seam

To obtain pattern for pop-over, lay tracing paper over pattern pieces and trace printed outlines. Cut out new pattern.

Shoulder Seam

Side Seam

Back

Loop

Loop

Center Back

37

Fashion Flair
Frog fastenings

Frog fastenings are big fashion news when used on long coats, casual belts, separates, tunic suits, or evening clothes. Use these simple step-by-step directions for making your own basic frog pattern, then try experimenting with other, more elaborate designs.

Materials
Soutache braid and round braid (which you can buy), and self-filled or corded tubing (which you can make), are all suitable for making frogs, as they are flexible and will bend without distorting.

Separately-made frogs
Using either the frog pattern given below (Figure 1), or your own choice of shape, trace the outline onto a sheet of paper. Starting at point A (Figure 2), form the braid into the required shape by following the outline you have drawn (Figures 3, 4, 5 and 6). Catch the braid together with tiny stitches where it overlaps. If the frogs are elaborate, stick them to the paper with Scotch tape while sewing. Trim the raw end of the braid, tuck it under the join of the second loop of the frog, and sew it neatly to the other end at point A. Attach the frogs to the garment with tiny stitches.

Figure 1

Frogs made on a garment
Mark the outline of the frog shape on the garment with basting stitches. Form the frog as above, catching the braid together with tiny stitches, and at the same time securing the frog to the garment.

Loop buttonholes
You can make a simple buttonhole either with a loop of braid or tubing, or by sewing a frog at the open edge of a coat (see photograph on the opposite page), using one of the loops as a buttonhole. This loop must be formed large enough to slip over the button easily.

Figure 2

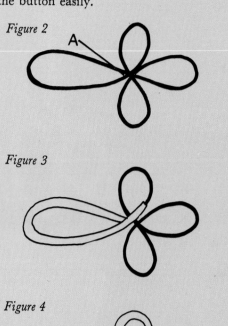

Figure 3

Figure 4

Figure 5

Figure 6

Chinese ball buttons

You can easily make these buttons from fine, round tubing to match the frogs. You will need 16 inches of tubing for each button. Loop it as shown in Figures 7, 8 and 9, keeping any seam lines uppermost. To close the button up, pull both ends of the tubing gently, easing the loops into each other. When the button is firm (Figure 10), snip off the ends of the tubing and join them together neatly at the back of the button. Sew the buttons to the garment with a short shank so that the frogs fasten neatly.

Figure 7

Figure 8

Figure 9

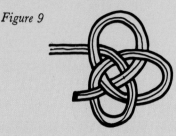

Figure 10

This beautiful coat shows how dramatic effects can be achieved by combining frogs with matching braid. They give a casual elegance to the simple lines of this hooded coat. ►

Figuring out the facts

Paper patterns are made to fit a variety of different figure types. Check your measurements against this chart to ensure that you always buy the right size for your figure.

Buy coat, dress and suit patterns by the correct bust measurement, as the bust is the hardest area to alter. For pants and skirt patterns, the waist measurement is the best guide; if, however, your hips are larger in proportion to your waist measurement, then purchase by the hip size, as the waist is easier to alter. If the pattern includes more than one garment, such as a blouse and pants, purchase by the bust size.

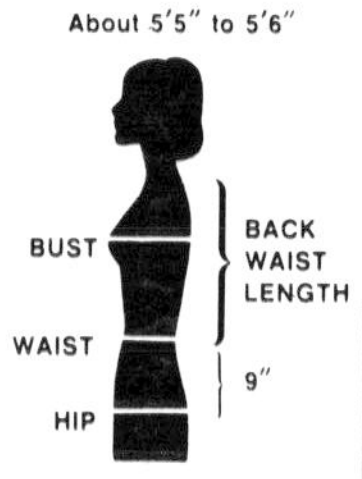

CREATIVE HANDS PATTERN PACK

The Pattern Pack is a set of versatile basic patterns for a blouse, dress and pants given in Volume 22 which adapt to make an 18-piece wardrobe. Check your sizing against the chart.

Size	32½	34	36	38	40	42
Bust	32½	34	36	38	40	42
Waist	24	25½	27	29	31	34
Hip	34½	36	38	40	42	44

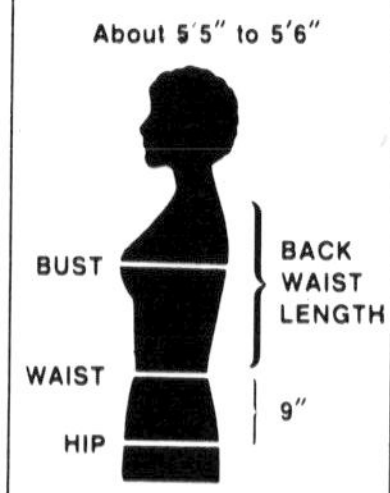

MISSES'
About 5′5″ to 5′6″

Designed for a well proportioned and developed figure; height about 5′ 5″ to 5′ 6″.

Size	6	8	10	12	14	16	18
Bust	30½	31½	32½	34	36	38	40
Waist	22	23	24	25½	27	29	31
Hip	32½	33½	34½	36	38	40	42
Back waist length	15½	15¾	16	16¼	16½	16¾	17

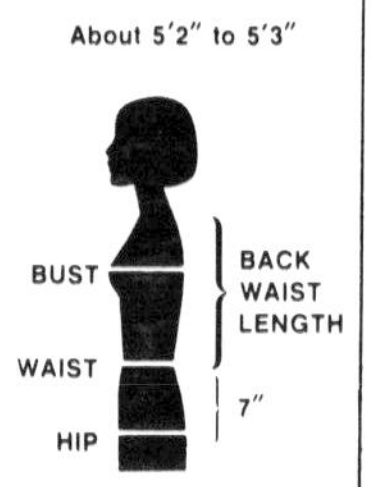

MISS PETITE
About 5′2″ to 5′3″

Designed for the shorter Miss figure; height about 5′ 2″ to 5′ 3″.

Size	6mp	8mp	10mp	12mp	14mp	16mp
Bust	30½	31½	32½	34	36	38
Waist	22½	23½	24½	26	27½	29½
Hip	32½	33½	34½	36	38	40
Back waist length	14½	14¾	15	15¼	15½	15¾

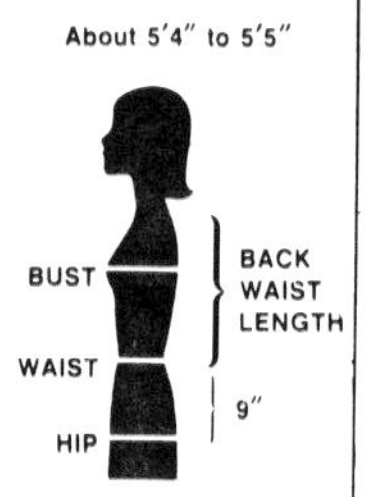

JUNIOR
About 5′4″ to 5′5″

Designed for a well-proportioned, shorter waisted figure; height about 5′ 4″ to 5′ 5″.

Size	5	7	9	11	13	15
Bust	30	31	32	33½	35	37
Waist	21½	22½	23½	24½	26	28
Hip	32	33	34	35½	37	39
Back waist length	15	15¼	15½	15¾	16	16¼

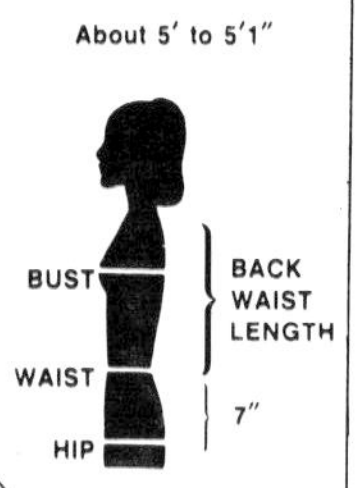

JUNIOR PETITE
About 5′ to 5′1″

Designed for a well-proportioned petite figure; height about 5′ to 5′ 1″.

Size	3jp	5jp	7jp	9jp	11jp	13jp
Bust	30½	31	32	33	34	35
Waist	22	22½	23½	24½	25½	26½
Hip	31½	32	33	34	35	36
Back waist length	14	14¼	14½	14¾	15	15¼

WOMEN'S
About 5′5″ to 5′6″

Designed for the larger, more fully mature figure; height about 5′ 5″ to 5′ 6″.

Size	38	40	42	44	46	48	50
Bust	42	44	46	48	50	52	54
Waist	34	36	38	40½	43	45½	48
Hip	44	46	48	50	52	54	56
Back waist length	17¼	17⅜	17½	17⅝	17¾	17⅞	18

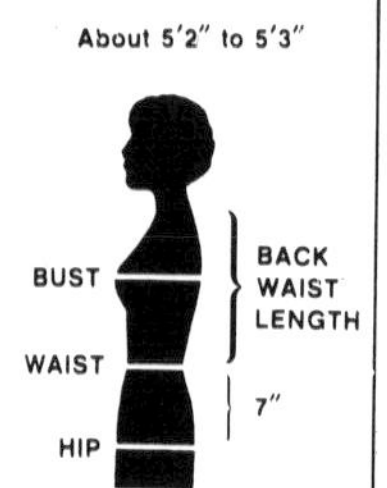

HALF-SIZE
About 5′2″ to 5′3″

Designed for a fully developed figure with a short back waist length. Waist and hip are larger in proportion to bust than other figure types; height about 5′ 2″ to 5′ 3″.

Size	10½	12½	14½	16½	18½	20½	22½	24½
Bust	33	35	37	39	41	43	45	47
Waist	26	28	30	32	34	36½	39	41½
Hip	35	37	39	41	43	45½	48	50½
Back waist length	15	15¼	15½	15¾	15⅞	16	16⅛	16¼

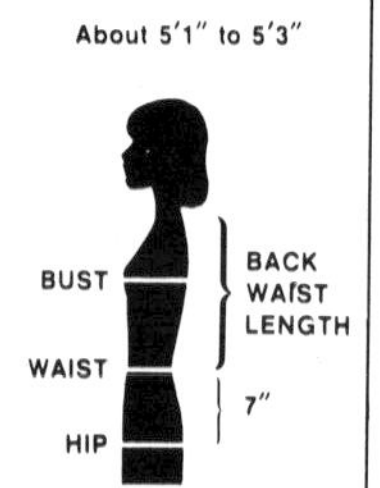

YOUNG JUNIOR/TEEN
About 5′1″ to 5′3″

Designed for the pre-teen and teen figures; height about 5′ 1″ to 5′ 3″.

Size	5/6	7/8	9/10	11/12	13/14	15/16
Bust	28	29	30½	32	33½	35
Waist	22	23	24	25	26	27
Hip	31	32	33½	35	36½	38
Back waist length	13½	14	14½	15	15⅜	15¾

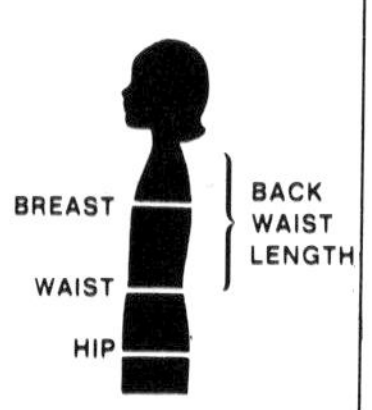

GIRLS'

Designed for the young girl who has not yet begun to mature.

Size	7	8	10	12	14
Breast	26	27	28½	30	32
Waist	23	23½	24½	25½	26½
Hip	27	28	30	32	34
Back waist length	11½	12	12¾	13½	14¼

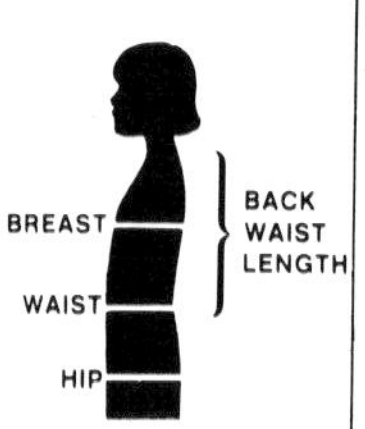

CHUBBIE

Designed for the young girl who is above the average size for her age.

Size	8½c	10½c	12½c	14½c
Breast	30	31½	33	34½
Waist	28	29	30	31
Hip	33	34½	36	37½
Back waist length	12	12¾	13½	14¼

Pattern Library

Every so often Pattern Library introduces a new design which is simple to copy or adapt. This illustration is almost life-size so that you can clearly count the threads and stitches. Use it on a cushion or a bag, or it would look charming worked on the hem of a dress with the design repeated and reversed. It could easily be adapted for needlepoint cushions or chair seats.

To copy the design, use an even-weave fabric with 16 threads to the inch. A finer fabric produces a smaller design—a coarser fabric, a larger one. Work it in cross-stitch and backstitch. Use four strands of six-strand embroidery floss in red, violet, yellow, bright blue, apricot, leaf green and ivy green.

Meet the basic stitches

Knitting Know-how 3

In knitting, there are only two basic stitches—knit and purl. A wide variety of patterns is possible using just one or a combination of both these stitches. And depending on the needles and yarn you choose, the texture of these patterns can range from smooth to heavy, or even be as light as lace!

How to join yarn

Always join yarn at the beginning of a row, never in the center, or it will spoil the continuity of the stitches. The only exception is when you are using circular or double-pointed needles, which will be featured in a later chapter. Leave a short length of yarn at the end of the row; begin the next row with the new yarn, again leaving a short end for darning in. Tie these ends together in a square knot. You can then darn these ends neatly into the edge when your knitting is finished.

How to measure

Never try to lay the work to be measured over your knee or along the arm of a chair. Be certain that you lay the knitting on a flat surface and that you measure with a non-stretch ruler rather than a tape. Do not include the cast-on edge in your measurement, but begin with the base of the first row. When measuring an armhole or sleeve, do not measure around the curve or up the sloping edge, but measure straight up the center of the fabric.

Every time you meet a new stitch, it's wise to make a 4in gauge swatch. When you've enough swatches, sew them up into a bright patchwork quilt!

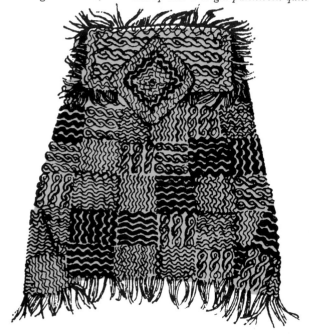

Knit stitch

1. Take the needle with the cast-on stitches in your left hand, and the other needle in your right hand. Insert the right-hand needle point through the first stitch on the left-hand needle from front to back.
Keeping the yarn away from you behind the needles, pass the yarn around the point of the right-hand needle so that you form a loop.
2. Draw this loop through the stitch on the left-hand needle, thus forming a new loop on the right-hand needle.
3. Allow the stitch on the left-hand needle to slip off.
Repeat these steps until you have drawn loops through all the stitches on the left-hand needle to the right-hand one. You have now knitted one row. To work the next row, change the needle holding the stitches to your left hand and the free needle to your right hand, and work this row in exactly the same manner as the first row.

Purl stitch

4. Take the needle with the cast-on stitches in your left hand, and the other needle in your right hand. Insert the right-hand needle point through the first stitch on the left-hand needle from back to front. Keeping the yarn toward you in front of the needles, pass yarn around point of right-hand needle to form a loop.
5. Draw this loop through the stitch on the left-hand needle, thus forming a new loop on the right-hand needle.
6. Allow the stitch on the left-hand needle to slip off.
Repeat these steps with the next stitch, until you have drawn loops through all the stitches on the left-hand needle and passed them onto the right-hand needle.
You have now purled one row. Change the needles, and work other rows in the same way. If you practice knitting and purling, you will find that you become faster and that your work becomes much more even and regular.

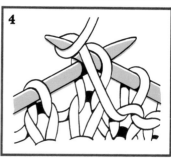
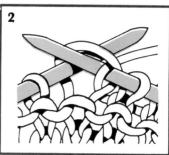
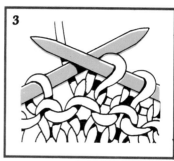
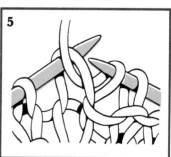
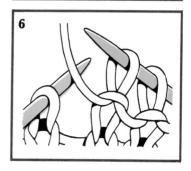

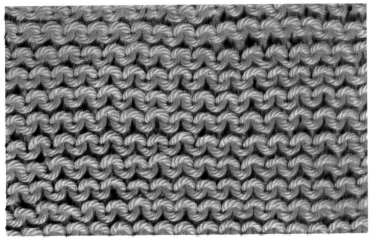

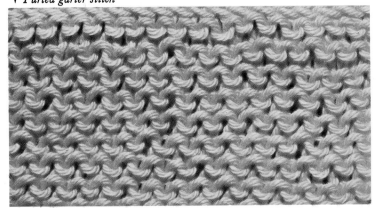

▲ *Knitted garter stitch*
▼ *Purled garter stitch*

When the scarf is completed, you can muffle up against the weather

Garter stitch

This is the simplest of all the knitting patterns, formed by working every row in the same stitch, either knit or purl.

If you purl every row, however, you will not get as smooth or even a surface as when you knit every row. This is because all knitters knit more evenly than they purl. So, whenever you come across directions referring to garter stitch, it is intended that you knit every row, unless otherwise specified.

Stockinette stitch

This is the smoothest of all the patterns in knitting and is made by alternately knitting one row and purling the next. The knit side of the work in stockinette stitch is usually called the right side. If the pattern uses the purl side as the right side, it is then called reversed stockinette stitch.

▼ *Stockinette stitch*

Beginners — continuing your scarves

Having cast on 50 sts for the woman's scarf or 30 sts for the child's scarf, you are now ready to start knitting.

To make: Work in garter stitch (knit every row) until 70in (50in) from beg, or desired length.

You can, of course, make either scarf shorter or longer if you like. Remember, you will need to buy more yarn if you want to make the scarf longer.

Don't be tempted to press your scarf at any stage. Garter stitch should always be treated like velvet—never pressed or flattened. If by any chance this warning is too late and the harm is already done, it can quite easily be repaired. Hold the scarf in the steam from a steadily boiling kettle, and the damp heat will rapidly raise the flattened wool fibers back to their original springiness.

Knitting Know-how 4: Bind off and fringe your scarf

A 3-piece set to knit

Keep baby snug in this suit of soft creamy yarn. The pullover with a comfortable collar and easy center front opening is knitted in an interesting textured stitch with garter stitch edgings. The garter stitch leggings have simple ribbed feet to do away with complicated shaping. Traditionally, babies wear pink, blue or white, but for fun try white with navy leggings and pompon.

Sizes
Directions are for size 6 months Pullover, length at center back, 10 [11:12½] in
Sleeve seam, 7 [8:9] in
Leggings, length from top to beginning of foot ribbing, 16 [17½: 19] in, adjustable
The figures in brackets [ ] refer to the 1 year and 2 year sizes respectively

Gauge
6 stitches and 8 rows to one inch over stockinette stitch on No.5 needles

Materials shown here
Sports Yarn
10 [12:14] ounces
One pair No.3 needles or Canadian No.10
One pair No.5 needles or Canadian No.8
Set of four No.5 or Canadian No.8 double-pointed needles
Three buttons
Waist length of elastic

Pullover back
Using No.3 needles cast on 50 [56:62] sts.

Work 5 rows garter st.
Change to No.5 needles.

Commence patt.
1st row P2, *yo, K1, yrn, P2, rep from * to end.
2nd row K2, *P3, K2, rep from * to end.
3rd row P2, *K3, P2, rep from * to end.
4th row K2, *ytf, sl 1P, P2 tog, psso, ytb, K2, rep from * to end.
These 4 rows form patt and are rep throughout.
Continue in patt until work measures 6 [6½:7½] in from beg, ending with a 4th patt row.

Shape armholes
Bind off 6 sts at beg of next 2 rows.
Continue without shaping until armhole measures 4 [4½:5] in from beg, ending with a WS row.

Shape shoulders
Bind off 7 sts at beg of next 2 rows.
Bind off 5 [7:9] sts at beg of next 2 rows.
Bind off rem sts.

Front

Work as given for back until front measures 4½ [5:6] in from beg, ending with a 4th patt row.

Divide for front opening
Next row Patt on 22 [25:28] sts, bind off 6 sts, patt to end.
Complete right side first.
Continue in patt until front measures same as back to underarm, ending at armhole edge.

Shape armhole
Bind off 6 sts at beg of next row, patt to end.
Continue without shaping until armhole measures 2in, ending at center front edge.

Shape neck
Dec one st at neck edge on next 4 [5:6] rows.
Continue without shaping until armhole measures same as back to shoulder, ending at armhole edge.

Shape shoulder
Bind off at armhole edge 7 sts once, then 5[7:9] sts once.
With WS of work facing attach yarn to rem sts and complete to match first side.

Sleeves (two alike)

Using No.3 needles cast on 29 [32:35] sts.
Work 5 rows garter st.
Change to No.5 needles.
Work in patt as for back, inc one st at each end of 7th and every following 8th row until there are 37 [42:47] sts.
Continue without shaping until work measures 7 [8:9] in from beg, ending with a WS row.

Shape cap
Bind off 6 sts at beg of next 2 rows and 3 [4:5] sts at beg of following 6 rows.
Bind off rem sts.

Borders

Using No.3 needles cast on 8 sts. Work 1¼in garter st.
Next row K3, bind off 2, K3.
Next row K3, cast on 2, K3.
Make 2 more buttonholes in this way at intervals of 1in.
Continue until border measures 3½in from beg.
Bind off.
Make another border in same way, omitting buttonholes.

Collar

Using No.5 needles cast on 41 [47:53] sts.
Rep patt rows as given for back 4 [4:5] times.
Bind off.

Finishing

STEAM LIGHTLY
Join shoulder, side and sleeve seams. Set in sleeves. Sew borders to center front opening and catch down at center front. Sew bound off edge of collar to neck, beg and ending at center of borders. Sew on buttons.

Leggings left leg

Using No.3 needles cast on 52 [58:64] sts.
Work 3 rows K1, P1 rib.
Next row Rib 1, *yrn, work 2 tog, rep from * to last st, rib 1.
Work 4 more rows in rib.
Change to No.5 needles.
Continue in garter st.

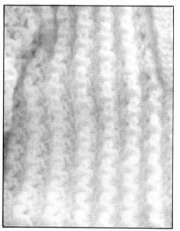

▲ *Close-up of textured stitch*

Shape back (short rows)
Next row K15, turn, K to end.
Next row K30, turn, K to end.
Next row K45, turn, K to end.
Continue across all sts until garter st measures 1 [1½:2] in.
Inc one st at each end of next and every following 14 [16:18]th row until there are 60 [66:72] sts.
Work 10 rows without shaping.
Dec one st at each end of next and every other row until 48 [52:60] sts rem, then every following 6th row until 28 [32:40] sts rem.
Work a further 2 [2½:3½] in without shaping, or until required leg length to foot ribbing.
Divide sts on 3 of the set of 4 No.5 needles and work around in K1, P1 rib for 4 [4½:5] in.

Shape toe

Next round Sl 1, K2 tog, psso, rib 7 [9:13], K3 tog, P1, sl 1, K2 tog, psso, rib 7 [9:13], K3 tog, P1.

Work 2 rounds without shaping.

Next round Sl 1, K2 tog, psso, rib 3 [5:9], K3 tog, P1, sl 1, K2 tog, psso, rib 3 [5:9], K3 tog, P1.

Work 2 rounds without shaping.

Weave rem sts tog.

Leggings right leg

Work as given for left leg, reversing back shaping.

Finishing

STEAM LIGHTLY

Join leg seams. Join front and back seams. Thread elastic through holes at waist and join together to fit.

Hat

Using No.5 needles cast on 80 [80:86] sts.

Work 5 rows garter st.

Work 3 complete patts as given for pullover back.

Next row K.

Beg with a 1st patt row.

Continue until work measures 7 [7½:8] in from beg, ending with a 4th patt row.

Shape top

Next row *P2 tog, K1; rep from * to last 2 sts, P2 tog.

Change to No.3 needles and continue in garter st.

Work 5 rows.

Next row *K2, K2 tog, rep from * 12 [12:13] times more, K1.

Work 5 rows without shaping.

Next row *K1, K2 tog, rep from * 12 [12:13] times more, K1.

Thread yarn through rem sts, draw up and fasten off.

Finishing

STEAM LIGHTLY

Join side seams tog.

Make a pompon and sew to top of hat.

All set to go out ▶

Lots of new stitches to try

Once you have learned the techniques of the double and treble stitches shown on these pages, you will find yourself able to create a whole new array of lovely articles. These stitches, so easy to master and so quick to crochet, will be of interest to all. Almost effortlessly there is satisfaction, as you see your work grow rapidly row by row.

The unusual belt shown on the opposite page is just one way of using crocheted rounds. With this method you can make a variety of things, from place mats to handbags to shawls, or even a lacy dress. And, of course, any one of these items would make a delightful gift.

Variations of the double stitch

1. Short double (sdc) or half double (hdc)

Make the required length of chain.

1st row. Skip first 2ch, * yoh, insert hook into next ch, yoh, draw through one stitch (3 loops on hook), yoh, draw through all loops on hook (1 loop on hook), (this makes 1 sdc), repeat from * to end of ch. Turn.

2nd row. 2ch, * 1 sdc into next sdc, rep from * to last sdc, 1 sdc into 2nd of 2 turning ch. Turn. Rep 2nd row for length required.

2. Treble stitch (tr)

To begin, first work the required length of chain.

1st row. Skip first 4ch, * yarn twice over hook—called y2oh— insert hook into next ch, yoh, draw loop through ch, yoh, draw loop through first 2 loops on hook, yoh, draw loop through next two loops on hook, yoh, draw loop through last 2 loops on hook, (this makes 1 tr), rep from * to end of ch. Turn.

2nd row. Work 4ch. Work 1 tr into next tr, rep from * to end of row, working last tr into 4th ch or turning ch. Turn. Rep 2nd row for length required.

3. Double treble (dtr)

Work these stitches in the same way as treble, passing the yarn over hook three times, instead of twice. Then work the loops off in the same way, two at a time, until one loop remains on hook.

4. Double around double

This stitch is frequently used in designs where a deeply ridged effect is required. Make the ridge by working around the double in the previous row, instead of working into the chain at the top of the stitches. Shown below is a sample of double already worked, with the hook in position to work the next stitch around the double in the previous row. The ridge is made by the top chain on the previous row being left free on the reverse side of the work.

5. Double between double

To crochet with the stitches alternating more definitely, work into the space between the doubles in the previous row. The illustration shows ordinary double with the hook in position to work the next double into the space in the previous row.

The last two stitches show how you can change the appearance of a familiar stitch by varying the way you insert the hook.

▼ *Short double (sdc) or half double (hdc) stitch*

▼ *Double around double stitch*

▼ *Treble stitch (tr)*

▼ *Double between double stitch*

▲ *Single crochet*

crochet stitches, the thickness of the yarn chosen can alter the whole appearance, so keep in mind the effect you want.

To make shapes like circles, rosettes, ovals and squares, begin in the middle of the shape and work outwards to the edge, instead of the usual method of working in rows. As a rule, the same basic method is used.

Make the central circle from a short chain, looped around to form a circle and joined by 1 ss into the first ch. Into this first circle work twice the number of stitches of the original chain and complete the round by joining to the first stitch with a ss. Shape is made in the next rounds by the position of the increased stitches.

Slip stitch (ss)

This stitch is used chiefly for joining or in intricate patterns, and it is the shortest in height of all the crochet stitches.

Make the required length of chain.

1st row. Skip first ch, * pass hook through top loop of next ch, yoh, draw yarn through both stitches on hook, rep from * to end of ch. Turn. This makes 1 slip stitch (ss).

2nd row. Ch 1, * 1 ss into next ss, rep from * working last ss into turning ch of previous row.

Repeat second row for length required. Fasten off.

Crocheting around

This method produces the most beautiful results, from the simplest form of colorful American Granny squares (shown in chapter 1) to the finest cobweb look of traditional Irish crochet. As with all

Making a belt

This unusual belt is very simple to make. It's just a series of small circles stitched together and tied with a braided cord and tassels in matching or contrasting color.

Size: Each circle is about 1½ inches in diameter.

Materials: You will need about 4 yards of knitting worsted for each circle and No. E (3.50 mm) crochet hook.

To make each circle

Work 3ch, join into a circle with 1 slip stitch into first ch.

1st round. Work 6sc in circle, joining to first sc with ss.

2nd round. Work 2sc in each sc of previous round. Join with ss (12sc).

3rd round. As 2nd round (24sc).

4th round. * Work 2sc in next sc, 1 sc in next sc, rep from * to end. Join with ss (36sc). Fasten off.

Finishing

Join the circles as shown in the illustration using contrasting or matching yarns. Braid together several strands of yarn to form cords for tying and sew to the back of the end circles.

▼ *Joining chain to form a circle*

▼ *The disc when almost complete*

▼ *Here's a fascinating belt of discs that is easy to crochet*

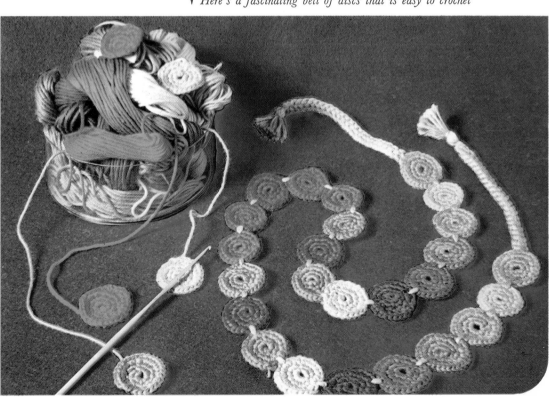

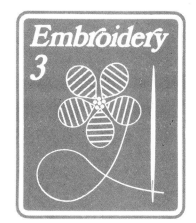

Don't ignore the simple line stitches

If you are new to embroidery, running stitches will provide a sound basis for developing your embroidery skills. These are the easiest embroidery stitches to work. They all form lines—useful for outlining shapes, embroidering curved stems and working geometrical designs. Although running stitches are simple, they should not be ignored, as they form exciting patterns when used imaginatively. Like many other simple stitches, they can be used as the basis of more elaborate techniques.

An interesting idea for trying out the stitches would be to make a sampler or a wall hanging on coarse natural colored burlap. Work the stitches large and bold in a fascinating mixture of textures such as raffia, string, nubbly and fluffy yarn, all in shades of natural and creamy white with small touches of one contrasting color. The edges of the burlap could then be fringed or simply bound with a plain hem, and the whole sampler hung from a chunky bamboo pole.

Long and short running stitch
Work in the same way as running stitch but make the upper stitches alternately long and short, the short ones being equal in length to the stitches underneath.

Backstitch
Working from right to left, bring the needle through to the right side of the cloth and make a small stitch backward. Then bring the needle through again a little in front of the first stitch and take another backstitch to the front of the first stitch. Continue working across.

Backstitch—doubled
Make a stitch backward as for backstitch. Then, instead of bringing the needle through again in front of this stitch, bring it through where you started and make the stitch over again.
Continue as for backstitch, working each stitch twice.

Outline stitch
This is rather like backstitch, but is worked from left to right.
Make a slightly sloping stitch along the line of the design, and then take the needle back and bring it through again about halfway along the previous stitch, on the lower side.

Laced and whipped running stitch

Running stitch can be laced or whipped to give extra effect, either with the same or a contrasting colored thread. Take a tapestry needle and thread it in and out of the stitches as shown on the opposite page, without letting it catch in the cloth. Running stitch is used in the diagrams, but these techniques can be used equally well with backstitch.

Long and short running stitch

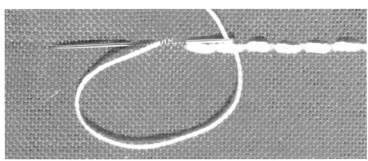

Backstitch

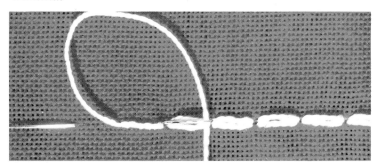

Backstitch—doubled

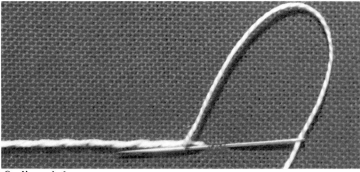

Outline stitch

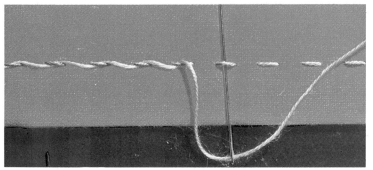

Running stitch looks more exciting when it is whipped

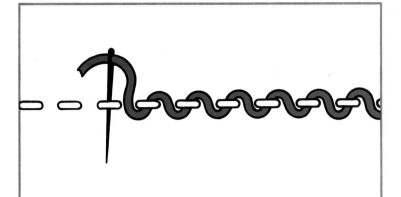

Whipped running stitch

Laced effect

Double lacing

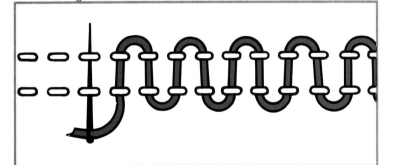

Interlacing

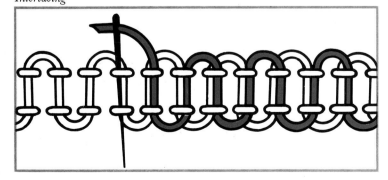

Double interlacing

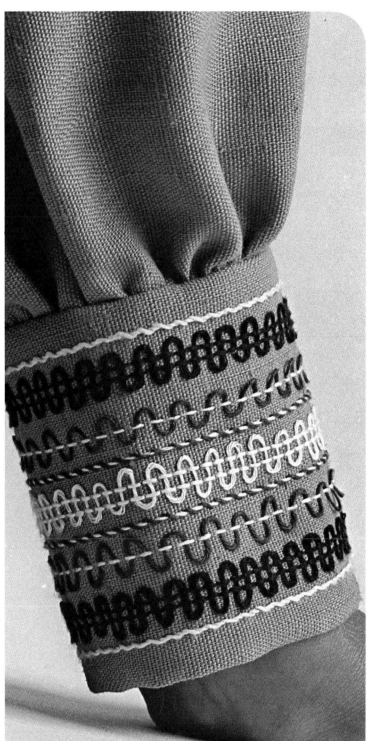

Borders bright and beautiful

Just look at this lovely embroidered cuff. Stunning, isn't it!
You can easily do it yourself as it's made up of a combination
of stitches illustrated in this chapter. Try it on cuffs or collars,
sleeves or yokes—and wouldn't it look pretty worked around the
hem of a little girl's skirt?
It isn't necessary to follow the pattern shown here. You can make
up your own individual design and color scheme. But remember
—for a sophisticated, high fashion effect, use only one or two
colors at a time to let the stitches make their full impact. For a
peasant effect, however, the more colorful the better!

Make a mitered tablecloth

Tablecloths no longer create the laundering problems our grandmothers had. With the easy-care fabrics now available, you can make drip-dry cloths in colors to match your china, window shades, curtains, or even wallpaper. If the surface of your dining table needs protection from hot plates, you can buy heat-proof material, cut it into the exact size of the table top, and put it underneath the cloth. Use the directions given here to make a plastic tablecloth—more practical than fabric if there are children around, as you can just wipe it down whenever food is spilled. Sew braid or fringe around the edges to make it look pretty, or sew a panel down the center for a bold, contrasting effect.

What you need
☐ Fabric for the tablecloth
☐ Sewing thread to match
☐ Trimmings

Measure the top of your table and buy sufficient material to allow for a generous amount to hang down on the four sides. (About 10–14in on each side for an average size rectangular table.) For a plain hem you should allow another 2in all around, but if you are planning a fringe or ball fringe edging then ½in extra is sufficient.

How to make a cloth

If the material you are using is not wide enough to be made up into a tablecloth in one piece, join the separate widths of fabric using either a plain seam or flat fell seam. If you are using a fairly sheer fabric such as a voile or other fine cotton, a flat fell seam is more suitable than a plain seam because with this seam all the raw edges are hidden.

For a plain edge turn under a 1½in hem. Miter the corners and hand-sew or machine stitch all around for the edges.

For a trimmed edge turn over the fabric ½in on the right side and pin and baste the trimming to cover the raw edge. Sew along the top and the bottom of the trimming to secure it.

Making seams a feature

If you have to make your cloth out of more than one piece there are several ways of making a special feature out of joining widths of fabric. Usually it looks best if you join the fabric in two seams so that there is a panel running down the center of the cloth. With a stripe you can cut the central panel so that the stripes run in the opposite direction to the main piece of fabric.

A small floral print can be joined by a plain seam on the right side, the seam edges trimmed to ¼in of the stitching line and the raw edges covered with a braid or ribbon. A plain linen cloth can be made very unusual by applying some of the simple embroidery stitches shown in this week's Embroidery chapter.

To miter a corner
1. Fold over the raw edges ½in and press. Make another fold 1½in from each folded edge and press again firmly. Now open out these folds and turn in the corner on a diagonal line at the point where the two previous fold lines meet. Press firmly to make a crease.

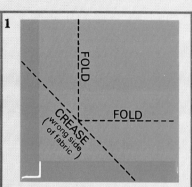

2. Trim off the corner to ¼in from the diagonal crease, cutting firmly through the turned-in raw edges. Fold at right angles to the trimmed edge right sides together, and sew along the crease line from the point to the folded edge. Turn right side out and gently ease out the point with a knitting needle.

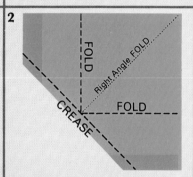

3. Now refold the 1½in hems already pressed over, pin and baste all around. Machine stitch close to the edge or hand sew with a neat slip stitch. Press tablecloth on the wrong side, taking care not to iron over the double thickness along the edge or it will leave a line on the right side.

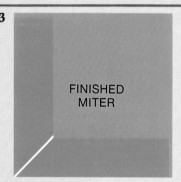

FINISHED MITER

Plain seam
With right sides together, machine stitch or backstitch by hand ½in from the edge of the fabric.

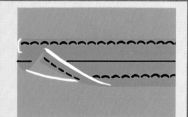

Finishing seams
To make neat edges either use the zigzag on your machine, or turn under the raw edge of the seam allowance and machine stitch close to the edge.

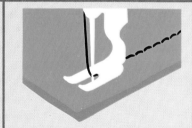

Flat fell seam
Join as for a plain seam, and trim one side of the seam allowance ¼in from the stitching line. Turn over the raw edge of the other side and fold over trimmed edge. Baste and machine stitch near the edge.

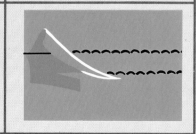

Lattice fringe and tassels

Following the simple knot, it is an easy step to learn how to make flat knots and tassels, which is what this chapter is all about. The flat knot for fringing looks intricate, but is easy to work when you know how. The center threads act as a core around which the outside threads are knotted in what every ex-Girl Scout or Brownie will recognize as a reef knot. All flat knots are worked in the same manner but over a varying number of threads.

Also in this chapter there are two simple fringes incorporating flat knots and tassels. Once you have learned how to make fringes, you can use them to give your own distinctive touch to all sorts of household items and to clothing. The drawings on the opposite page give several suggestions on how to adapt garments by adding a tasseled fringe.

The flat knot

Prepare the lengths of yarn as required and thread on in four evenly spaced bunches. The two center bunches act as a core over which the right and left bunches are knotted.

Hold the two center bunches taut by winding them around the third finger of the left hand. With the right hand, take the right-hand bunch under the center core and over the left-hand bunch. Then bring the left-hand bunch over the center core and thread it from the front through the loop formed by the right-hand bunch and the center core. Let go of the core, and pull the right- and left-hand bunches until they tighten around the center core. This completes the first stage of the knot.

For the second stage, once again holding the center core taut, pass the left-hand bunch under the core and over the right-hand bunch. Then take the right-hand bunch over the core and, from the front, thread it through the loop formed by the left-hand bunch and center core. Pull the ends tightly.

Tassels

Tassels for simple knot fringe patterns are formed out of the threads which remain after a pattern has been worked (see Fringing chapter 1). The tassels shown here consist of separate bundles of threads, doubled over and bound with separate threads. They are simple to make and ideal for using with flat knot fringes, as they can be worked in with the last flat knot of the pattern.

Making the tassel with a flat knot
Cut and prepare a bundle of threads for the tassel. Finish fringe pattern by working the first stage only of the last flat knot. Take the bundle of threads and work the second stage of the flat knot over the center of the bundle. Double over the bundle, bind with a separate thread, and secure at the back with a firm knot. Take the ends of tying thread into the center of the tassel and lose them.

Lattice fringe

Prepare lengths of yarn, as required, and thread on in bunches at half inch intervals.

1st row. Work a simple knot on the first bunch of threads, skip 2 bunches, work a simple knot on the next bunch. Repeat to end of row.

2nd row. Work a row of flat knots using 4 bunches of threads for each knot.

3rd row. * Work simple knots on each bunch of threads to the end of the row.

4th row. Divide each of the bunches in half and make basket weave squares as shown in the illustration.

5th row. Reassemble original bunches of thread and work simple knots on each.

6th row. Work a row of flat knots using 4 bunches of threads for each knot *.

Repeat from * to * until you reach the length you need.

Finish off with tassels, as required.

Two-tone chain fringe (yellow and red)

Prepare bunches of yarn in two colors and thread on in groups of 4 as follows: 1 bunch (yellow); 1 bunch (red); 1 bunch (red); 1 bunch (yellow). Space each group at one inch intervals.

1st row. Work flat knots on each group of 4 bunches to secure threads to the edge.

2nd row. Work flat knots below each of the previous ones, leaving the outside (yellow) bunches slack between the knots to form the loops of the vertical chain motif.

3rd row. As 2nd row.

4th row. *Take the outside bunches (yellow) of each group and work simple knots between them, linking one group to the next.

5th row. Work another row of simple knots below the previous ones.

6th row. Divide the threads coming from the simple knots and make 1 flat knot on each of the original groups of 4 bunches.

7th and 8th rows. As 2nd row *.

Repeat from * to * until you reach the length you need.

Finish off with tassels, as required.

Four bunches knotted onto an edge and worked to make a flat knot

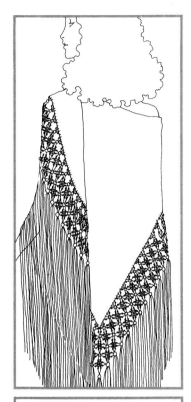

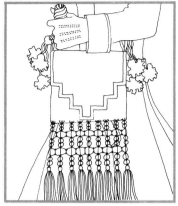

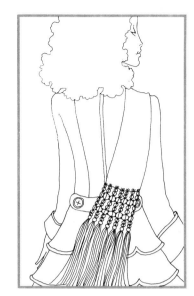

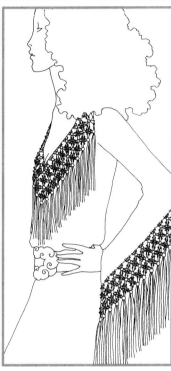

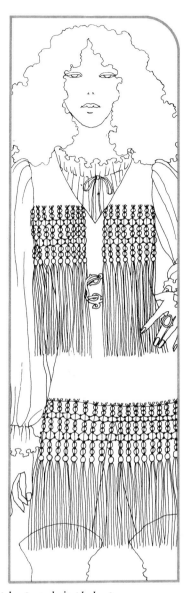

Here are several ideas for you to copy, using a lattice fringe and a two-tone chain fringe. If at all possible, work the fringe directly onto the material. If the fabric is not suitable, make a crocheted chain the required length and use this as a base from which to work. Then sew the fringe onto the article.

Lattice fringe with simple knots, flat knots and basket weave squares

Two-tone chain fringe made up of flat knots and simple knots

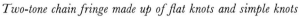

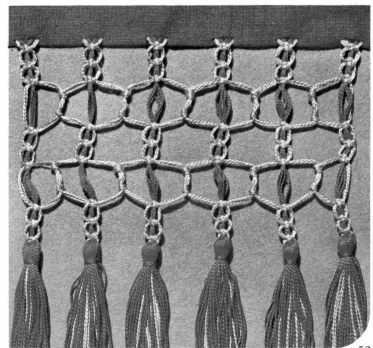

Coming to grips with your figure

Many people make their own clothes so that they can obtain a personal and distinctive look. One of the major advantages, however, is being able to achieve a perfect fit, which is so important for a really good-looking garment. So, before you start making your own clothes, it is essential that you identify your own personal figure type and are aware of any problems you may have. You can then select styles which flatter your figure, making the most of your good points and drawing attention away from your faults.

Most of us have figure problems. Sometimes it is merely a matter of bad posture which can be corrected with a little practice, but in fact very few people have such a perfect figure that they do not need to adapt designs or alter paper patterns in order to make them fit correctly.

If you work on the basis that almost any design can be adapted to any figure (except in extreme forms of fashion), all you have to do is recognize your own particular size and figure problem and take them into consideration when cutting out and fitting the garment. Naturally certain styles will be more flattering to one figure than to another.

In this chapter we have given suggestions with each of the three main figure types, to help you make the most suitable choice of style and fabric. With this knowledge, you can create a perfect picture whatever your figure problem, and feel really confident that your whole appearance is pleasing.

Which type are you?

There are three main figure types, which the chart on these pages illustrates: the figure with standard body measurements, the figure with a large bust and the figure with large hips. You'll be able to identify yourself with one of these whether you're tall or short, small or large or anywhere in between.

To find out which figure type you are, stand in front of a mirror, perfectly relaxed, just wearing your normal under garments and compare yourself to the figures illustrated.

What is your problem?

Having decided which figure type you are, you may then find you have particular figure problems like narrow, very straight or sloping shoulders, a rounded back, high tummy or a neck that's set forward. Some figure problems need special attention, and affect your choice of style as well as requiring careful fitting, while others are only a matter of making minor alterations to your pattern and do not greatly affect the style of dress you should choose.

The two most common figure problems, which involve adaptation of style, are illustrated on the facing page, with suggestions for choosing suitable styles. All fitting problems will be dealt with in more detail in later chapters.

Standard body measurements

The figure of standard proportions has a bust two inches smaller than the hip measurement. So, whatever your size, if you have this proportion, standard sizes will fit you without much alteration.

The choice of your clothes will depend on your height and whether you are broad or slim. If you are slim, perfectly proportioned and of average height, you are lucky and can wear almost anything you like. If you are large, wear garments that fit to the body, with well-fitting shoulders, as unnecessary bulk increases the impression of size. Avoid horizontal stripes and gathered, full skirts. If you are short and plump, always aim to achieve an elongating effect in the way you dress. This does not depend on the length of a garment, but on the vertical design detail. If you wear a belt or separates, they should match. If you are tall and thin, soft styles, blouses, pleated, gathered or flared skirts, wide belts, tweeds and fluffy fabrics are all good for you.

Large bust

If your bust measurement is more than your hip measurement, you are top heavy and yours is merely a fitting problem. Buy patterns to fit your bust and take them in by the necessary amount at the hips. The best designs for you are those which minimize the width across the top. You should avoid any bulk such as gathers and folds, shoulders should fit well and fabrics over the bust should be smooth. Scoop or 'V' necklines, which break up the area, are most effective on your figure type. If your hips are really slim, then you will look good in skirts made from tweeds and other heavily textured materials.

Figure Types

Figure Problems ▶

Large hips

The most feminine figure type is often referred to as pear-shaped. You are the girl with a good bust line and trim waist, but with larger than standard proportioned hips. To make your own clothes, buy patterns to fit your bust measurement and when you cut your garment, add to the width of the skirt pattern around the hips.

A-lines in skirts and dresses, and fitted bodices with full skirts are good for you. Remember that you will create an illusion of all-over smallness if you accentuate the smaller proportions of your top half and camouflage the fuller part of your body, especially if the outline of your garment flows into a little more width toward the hem. Straight skirts and dresses need very well-fitting blouses or bodices, perfectly plain and without too much ease. The soft blouse look is not the right style for you, unless you are really thin.

Rounded back, very sloping shoulders, a neck that is set forward and a high tummy

If this is your problem, your figure needs the very best support you can afford. Then it's a question of adapting the designs you choose.

As you appear narrow across the top and wide across the hips, triangular-shaped designs are ideal for you because they fit across your smallest points and skim over larger areas.

Never wear tuck-in blouses, but adapt them to short over-blouses, making sure that they are carefully proportioned to the length of your skirt.

Your neck is a very important point to watch because it will always appear short. Avoid high or large collars and aim for a neat, clear line. Adapt designs to a flat, fitting collar, a soft, narrow roll or even a plain, finished line around the base of your neck. If your neck is very thin, you can wear a close-fitting roll or mandarin collar if you like.

Bust larger than hips, flat tummy and very straight shoulders

If this is your problem, adapt the designs you choose. You will look best in fitted garments, without the bulk of gathers and folds. If you are broad or short, avoid waist seams and belts.

Always aim to minimize the width across the bustline, choosing soft, wide necklines on a straight, fitted dress. Keep trimming high above, or well below, the bustline. Draping should be used sparingly and be asymmetrical, leaving the bustline well-defined. A-line dresses (semi-fitted at waist and hips) will do nothing for you, since the line will be lost; but you can adapt this line to a fitted dress flared gently at the hem.

Make a point of choosing toning colors for your blouses and skirts and beware of shirt blouses, which can look very masculine on you.

Always choose a well-fitting shoulder line, with the armhole seam high on the shoulder to lessen the appearance of width. Avoid wide or short sleeves which will add to the width.

Fabric and design-how they go together

The first step toward making a dress for yourself is deciding on a style. Choose one in which you would like to see yourself, but study it carefully before buying the fabric.

Does the style suggest a soft line? Does it cling or does it drape? Does it have sculptured lines or geometric seaming? Does it suggest a tailored look or a more feminine outline? When choosing a fabric, always be guided by instinct and taste before taking anything else into consideration. Nothing is more frustrating than making a dress and finding the finished result is not as you imagined it would look. The reason for this, in many cases, is the wrong combination of fabric and style.

Use this guide to help you choose the right fabric for the style of dress you want to make.

56

Style	Clinging	Soft line	Draped
Detail	Soft and feminine, fitting closely to the body.	Unpressed pleats, gores or gentle flares.	Tight draping across the body, soft draping, cowl necks.
Fabric Suggestion	Plain knit jersey, lightweight silk or wool, crepe cut on the bias.	Soft or loosely woven fabrics, heavier crepe and jersey.	Lightweight crepe, chiffon, georgette and jersey.

Tailored,
sculptured,
geometric seaming

Design encloses
body in a
fitted, heavier
garment, or
holds a certain
shape dictated
by fashion.

Firm weaves
such as
worsted
woolen, real
or imitation
linen, heavy
cotton, double
knits, certain
man-made
fiber fabrics,
tweed and silk.

Prints and patterns

First, consider the style you have chosen and decide whether a printed or patterned fabric would be more suitable.

For the best results the style should be simple, because too much seam detail will break up the fabric design. Details such as belts, tabs or collars can be given clarity and look most effective in a plain fabric to match one color in the design. If you long for a beautifully seamed garment, this will always look best made up in a plain material.

Secondly, it's a good idea to drape a length of fabric over yourself in front of a mirror before you buy it, to see if the color really suits you.

Your choice of printed and patterned materials will, of course, be influenced by current fashion trends, but here are some hints on how to look at prints and patterns and make the best choice.

1. Two-color prints

On a printed fabric, the prominence of the design is an important factor. If the fabric is printed in two colors only,

the design appears to be balanced. Two-color prints are suitable for all figure types.

2. Three-color prints

As soon as a third color is introduced, and this need only be a different shading of the

two colors, the balance is broken and the design is immediately projected from the background. For instance, white daisies with navy centers on a navy background give the impression of overall interest. As soon as the center is picked out in yellow or any other color it is no longer just navy blue and white you see, but white daisies standing out from a dark background.

Three-color prints, or projected designs, can be worn by

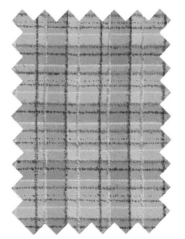

most figures, but if you are of large or small proportions do look carefully at the size of the design. A large design is more suitable for the larger figure, and a small design is more suitable for the smaller figure.

3. Directional prints

Large multi-colored prints can be worn successfully by most figures, but again if you are large or small, you must carefully consider the direction of the design. If you study the print from a distance, you'll see that one or two strong colors stand out from the

background and form the direction of the design, which can be round, oblong, diagonal, crisscross, vertical or horizontal. So, if you are large or short, the correct choice is the design which has continuous, lengthwise interest. This includes crisscross materials and diagonal prints.

4. Plaids, checks and stripes

When choosing plaids, checks and stripes, take into consideration your body movements when walking because brightly colored checks and plaids emphasize movement. Since body movement is relative to size, if you are large or short, be especially careful when looking at these fabrics. Large movements are emphasized by large checks and small movements drowned by them, so choose the smaller

patterns in blending colors if you are short.

As a point of interest, the large figure can wear bold, brightly colored plaids and checks to great effect, if the garments chosen are of generously cut design, such as travel coats or long evening skirts.

If you come across patterns with overchecks and outlines in bright, contrasting colors, always look at them from a distance. If your impression is of a large check or widely-spaced stripe, do remember this will determine the effect of the finished garment no matter how small the basic pattern is. Choose these fabrics with care and if you are large or short, avoid them altogether.

Pick your poncho

To get started on making your own clothes, here is a very simple garment for beginners—a poncho. Although it's so straightforward to make, it can be eye-catching, glamorous and very useful. According to the fabric you use, you can make a light, comfortable poncho to lounge in at home, or an unusual striking one for a more dressed-up effect. The poncho shown far left is simply a woolen square. All you have to do is fringe the edges and make an opening to slip over your head. What could be easier? The fitted poncho, shown on the opposite page, is slightly more complicated to make and has two seams, shoulder darts and applied fringe. It has a set outline which will keep its shape if made in a firmly woven fabric, and for extra warmth and firmness you can line it.

You may adapt the poncho by trimming with fur or braid instead of the fringe; by pattern darning a border; by making a 'poncho suit' with skirt or trousers; or by using an exciting upholstery fabric, or casual toweling for the beach.

Simple poncho

You will need $1\frac{1}{4}$yd of 54in wide wool fabric with warp and weft of equal strength. Sewing thread in a matching color.

To make the self-fringe

Trim the edges of the fabric on the grain and trim off selvages. Cut a 45in square. Along one edge of the square pull out the threads until you have a fringe two inches deep. Repeat on other three edges. To make certain that the inner edges do not fray, finish off with a tiny overcasting stitch between the fringing.

◀ *The simple poncho*

To make the neck opening

1. Lay on a flat surface and fold square, as shown, making sure that one triangle point is 3in lower than the other. This is for the back of the poncho.

2. Find the center of the fold from the side points and pin through both layers of fabric to the lower point of the triangle.

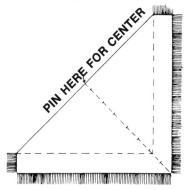

3. Fold on the pin line, making a 90° triangle. Pin edges.

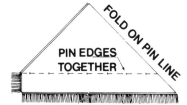

4. Measure around your head (as for hat) and divide by four. Find this measurement on the poncho with the tape measure by moving it down from the point, as shown. Pin a line across, shaping it into a curve. Cut off fabric close to the pins. Open out your poncho and turn under ½in around the hole. Baste, press and stitch.

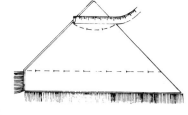

The fitted poncho ▲

Diagram for fitted poncho ►

This pattern darning design could be worked on the fitted poncho, all over or as a border. ▼

Fitted poncho

The poncho is made from two pieces of fabric 30in long and 15in wide, so you will need to buy ⅞yd of 36in or 54in wide, or ½yd of 60in wide fabric. Try it in a plain fabric with pattern darning, as illustrated. (The method is shown in Embroidery chapter 2.) You will also need 2⅝yd of ready-made fringe or, if you know how to make your own, you will need two balls of knitting yarn and matching thread.

Making the poncho

Cut fabric into two pieces 30in long and 15in wide.
Following the diagram, join the pieces together along AA and BB, right sides facing. Make ½in seams and stitch to within ½in of the neck edge.
If you want a snug fit over the shoulders, make two darts. To do this, turn the garment inside out and lay flat as shown in the illustration. Then, at each side of the neckline where the two folds fall, make a dart 3in wide, 3½in deep, as shown in the diagram. (Or, you can underlay the neckline with straight seam tape cut 1½in shorter than the neck edge, and ease the fullness into the seam tape at the shoulders.) Press the darts and carefully press the seams open.
To finish the neck edge, turn raw edge under ½in all around and hand sew to the inside. Finish the lower edge using the same method.
Sew fringe all around the lower edge of the poncho.

Lining the poncho

If you want to line the poncho, you should do this before you start to sew on the fringe.
Cut the lining fabric, join AA and BB and make darts exactly the same way as before. With right sides facing, join lining to top fabric all along the lower edge and turn right side out.
Turn in ½in on both neck edges separately and slipstitch the neck edges together.

Fashion Flair

Sew a pull-on jersey hat

Make this simple jersey cap in a couple of hours. Vary the look by making the brim in a contrasting color or the crown in two-tones, or pop on a sultry rose or a glossy bunch of cherries. Dress it up or down to suit your mood.

You will need
☐ ½yd wool or cotton jersey
☐ Matching sewing thread
☐ Tracing paper
☐ Pencil

Making the pattern
Trace the shape of the crown piece from the tracing pattern (Figure 1).
Cut out the shape.

60

Figure 1
Tracing pattern

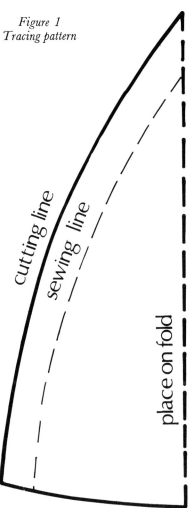

Cutting out the cap
From the ½yd of jersey, cut a strip 12½in wide and 23½in long. This is for the brim (Figure 2).
Cut 6 rectangles from the remaining fabric, each measuring 5½in by 5in, with the grain of the fabric running parallel with the 5½in side, as shown. These are for the crown pieces.

Figure 2

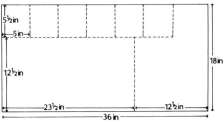

Fold one rectangle in half along the grain and pin the pattern to it (Figure 3).
Cut out the crown piece.
Cut out the other crown pieces in the same way.

Figure 3

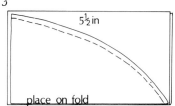

Making the cap
The crown. Place two crown pieces together, right sides facing, pin, baste and then machine stitch along the sewing line. Press the seam open. Repeat with the other two pairs of crown pieces. Join the pairs together as shown in Figure 4.
Press all the seams open and topstitch ¼in away from each seam (Figure 5).

Figure 4　　　*Figure 5*

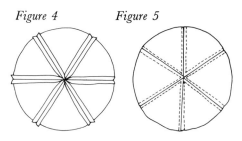

The brim. Fold the brim piece in half and machine stitch up the side as shown in Figure 6.
Press the seam open.

Figure 6

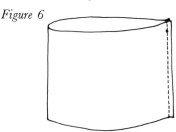

Joining the brim to the crown. Pin, baste and machine stitch the brim to the crown with a ½in seam allowance (Figure 7). Fold the brim down as shown in Figure 8 and press the seam carefully.
Topstitch around the seam.
Fold up ½in along the raw edge of the brim and press.

Figure 7　　　*Figure 8*

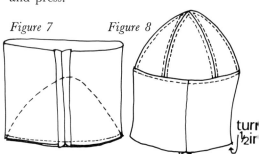

Turn the whole cap inside out and roll up the brim until the folded edge is just above the crown seam line. Pin, baste and hem the edge down (Figure 9). Topstitch around the lower edge of the brim.

Figure 9

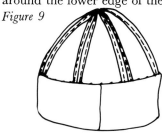

Cross-stitch alphabet

This alphabet chart has endless possibilities, as any 'square' stitch can be used. One square on the chart represents one stitch. Cross-stitch is the first that comes to mind, but beautiful initials can be worked in many other stitches. Fine, drawn fabric stitches such as four-sided stitch and eyelets can be worked on delicate lawn or fine linen. Bolder stitches, like satin stitch, eyelet filling or star stitch, are ideal on coarser cotton or linen. Stitches such as tent, Algerian eye, reversed cross, oblong cross and rice, are best for needlepoint.

An amusing idea is to make a cushion with a checkerboard background using two contrasting colors, such as vivid pink and lime green, then to build up a design by working letters of the alphabet in black in some of the squares. As a complete contrast in scale, you can use this alphabet to embroider fine initials on shirts, blouses or household linen. Scatter letters all over a little girl's blouse or dress — they could be the ones to make up her name. Then, use the alphabet to put your signature at the corner of anything you make. For small letters simplify the large ones which are shown on the chart. The following will be a guide to give you an idea of the approximate size of the letters worked on different fabrics: Using fine fabric, with 42 threads to 1in working over 4 threads, the letters will be $1\frac{1}{8}$in by 1in wide.

On coarser fabrics, with 21 threads to 1in working over 4 threads, the letters will be $2\frac{1}{4}$in by $1\frac{7}{8}$in wide.

On single weave canvas for needlepoint, with 18 threads to 1in working over 4 threads, the letters will be $2\frac{5}{8}$in by $2\frac{1}{4}$in.

Binding off and the slipped stitch

▲ *Slip stitch knitwise on a knit row*

This chapter starts with binding off. Gauge control is very important for this, as it must be done in exactly the same gauge as the knitting. If it is not, the edge will be too tight or too loose, and either will spoil the finished appearance of the garment. Slipped stitch is so called because it is slipped from the left-hand to the right-hand needle without being worked, the yarn being carried either behind or in front of the stitch. Slipped stitches can be used in several different ways— in forming part of a pattern in decreasing and shaping, in producing a neat edge for making up a garment, or in making a fold for a pleat or facing.

If you are working a pattern and the strand is passed behind the work, the stitch itself forms the pattern. If the strand is carried across the front of the stitch, then it can be used to build up the design, in much the same way as a woven design is made. You can also make fascinating herringbone textured effects using slipped stitches.

Binding off

To bind off on a knit row, knit the first two stitches. Then * with the left-hand needle point, lift the first stitch over the second stitch, leaving one stitch on right-hand needle. Knit the next stitch, repeat from * until all stitches but one have been worked off. Cut the yarn, draw through the last stitch and pull the stitch tight.

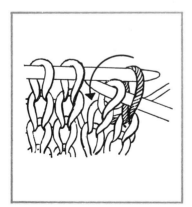

▲ *Lifting first stitch over second*

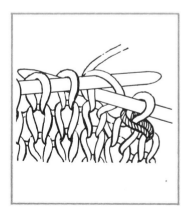

▲ *Knitting the next stitch*

When working a purl row, each stitch is purled before it is bound off. To bind off in pattern or ribbing, lift each stitch over the next stitch following the pattern of the knitting.

Care should always be taken that the binding off is not too tight or too slack, but is similar to the gauge of the work itself. If you always bind off too tightly, then use a needle one size larger for binding off. If, on the other hand, you bind off too loosely, use a needle one size smaller to obtain the best results.

Slipped stitches

Slip stitch knitwise on a knit row

Hold the yarn behind the work as if to knit the stitch. Insert the right-hand needle point into the stitch from front to back, as you would to knit, and slip it onto the right-hand needle.

Slip stitch purlwise on a knit row

Hold the yarn behind the work as if to knit the stitch. Insert the right-hand needle point into the stitch from back to front, as you would to purl, and slip it onto the right-hand needle.

Slip stitch purlwise on a purl row

Hold the yarn at the front of the work as if to purl the stitch. Insert the right-hand needle point from back to front as you would to purl, and slip it onto the right-hand needle.

It is most important to remember that when a slip stitch forms part of a decrease on a knit row, the stitch must be slipped knit-wise, otherwise it will become twisted. On a purl row, make sure you slip the stitch purlwise.

In working a pattern, however, when the slip stitch is not part of a decrease, it must be slipped purlwise on a knit row to prevent it from becoming twisted when purled in the following row. Don't forget to check which position you need for the best results.

▲ *Slip stitch purlwise on a purl row*

Fringe making

Take six strands of yarn and fold them in half. Draw the loop through the edge of the knitting, then draw the ends of the yarn through the loop and pull tightly. Repeat evenly all the way along the cast-on and bound-off edges of the scarf.

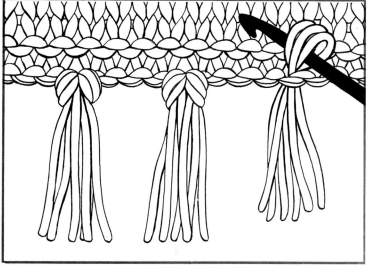

▲ *Drawing the loop through the edge of the knitting*

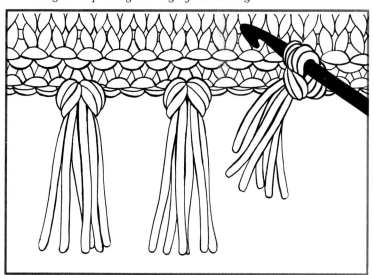

▲ *Drawing the ends of yarn through the loop*

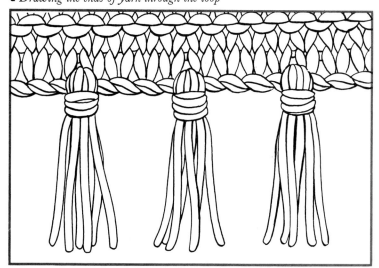

▲ *The fringe seen from the other side (usually called the right side)*

The fringed scarves when they are finished

Scarves for mother and child (continued)

You've just learned how to bind off—so now you can put it into practice. When you have finished binding off your scarf, you are ready to start working the fringe.

The garter stitch scarf in itself has no right or wrong side, but the first tassel dictates the pattern the rest must follow. Continue to work on the same side along the first end, being careful that the fringe is worked from the same side.

To make the fringe: Cut lengths of yarn 20in long for the mother's scarf, or 16in long for the child's scarf. You will need six strands for each tassel, and 16 tassels at each end of the mother's scarf, or 10 tassels at each end of the child's scarf. Use a crochet hook to pull the tassel loops through the edge of the scarf.

Knit a classic sweater for a man

This handsome crew neck pullover is a classic for the good reason that it is ideal for extra warmth without bulk. Try it in the bright red, or in any color that suits your taste (or his!). Just be sure the yarn you choose knits to the same basic gauge. The entire surface is simple ribbing, including the neckband, and the sweater has easy fitting, set-in sleeves.

Sizes

To fit a 36[38:40:42]in chest
Length to shoulder 25¾ [26:26¼:26½]in
Sleeve seam 20in (from wrist to underarm) adjustable
The figures in brackets [ ] refer to thè 38, 40 and 42in sizes respectively.

Gauge
Equivalent to a basic gauge of 5½ sts to one inch over stockinette stitch worked on No.7 needles.

Materials

Sports Yarn, 2oz skeins 9[10:11:12]
No.5 and No.7 needles or Canadian No.8 and No.6, or size necessary to obtain the gauge
Two stitch holders

Back

Using No.5 needles cast on 102[110:118:126]sts.
1st row K2, *P2, K2, rep from * to end.
2nd row P2, *K2, P2, rep from * to end.

Rep 1st and 2nd rows until work measures 4in.
Change to No.7 needles.
Continue in rib throughout
Work until 18in from cast on edge, or required length to underarm, ending with a WS row.

Shape armholes

Dec one st at each end of next and every RS row until 72[76:80:84]sts rem.
Work even until armholes measure 7¾[8:8¼:8½]in, ending with a WS row.

Shape shoulders

Bind off 5sts at beg of next 6 rows.
Bind off 4sts at beg of next 2 rows.
Bind off 4[5:6:7]sts at beg of next 2 rows.
Slip rem 26[28:30:32]sts onto a holder for the neckband.

Front

Work as given for back until armholes measure 5¾[6:6¼:6½] in, ending with a WS row.

Shape neck

1st row rib 29[30:31:32] sts, turn. Slip remaining sts on holder. Work left shoulder first.
** Dec one st at neck edge on next 4 rows, then on every RS row until 23[24:25:26] sts rem.
Work without shaping until armhole measurement is the same as back to shoulder measurement, ending at armhole edge.

Shape shoulder

At armhole edge, bind off 5sts every other row 3 times.
At armhole edge, bind off 4sts once; then 4[5:6:7]sts once. **
With RS of work facing, slip center 14[16:18:20]sts onto holder.
Rejoin yarn to rem sts and work in rib to end of row.
Work right shoulder as given for left shoulder, working from ** to **.

Sleeves (alike)

Using No.5 needles cast on 50[50:58:58]sts.
Work in rib as given for back until work measures 4in, ending with a WS row.
Change to No.7 needles.
Continue in rib, inc 1 st at each end of 3rd and every following 6th row until there are 84[88:92:96]sts.
Continue without shaping until work measures 20in or required seam length, ending with a WS row.

Shape cap

Dec one st at each end of next and every RS row until 54sts rem. Bind off in rib.

Neckband

Join left shoulder seam.
With RS of work facing and No.5 needles K 26[28:30: 32]sts from back neck holder, pick up and K 20 sts down left side of neck, K14 [16:18:20]sts from center front holder and pick up and K 20 sts up right side of neck.
1st row *K2, P2, rep from * to end.
Rep this row until neckband measures 2½in.
Bind off loosely in rib.

Finishing

Join right shoulder seam and neckband. Press all pieces lightly under a dry cloth with a cool iron. Join side and sleeve seams. Set in sleeves. Fold neckband in half to WS and slip st in place.

▼ This detail shows the knit two, purl two pattern

The sweater in two-by-two rib ►

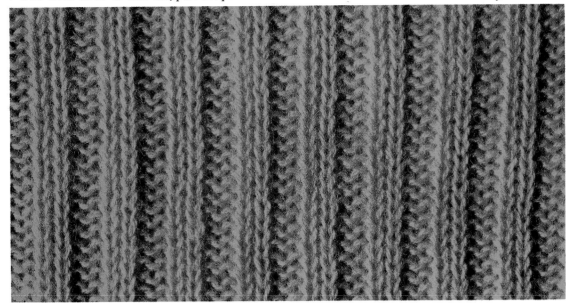

Increase or decrease

Knowing how to increase and decrease stitches is an important step in crochet, but one that becomes very simple with just a little practice. Once you master the methods, you can tackle almost any crochet item. Try the pillow cover shown and prove it!

Increasing

1. The simplest way to increase is to work two stitches into one. This can be done at each end of a row, or at one end only.
2. The second method is to add as many chains as the number of stitches to be increased, plus the turning chain at the end of the row. This way, an increase at the left side of the work is made at the end of a right side row, and an increase at the right side of the work is made at the end of a wrong side row. When the work is turned, the new chain is worked the same as a starting chain.
3. Mark the place where the increase is to be made with a length of colored thread. If the increase is to be made to the right, work two stitches into the stitch before the marker.
4. If the increase is to be made to the left, work these stitches into the stitch after the marker.
If the increases are to be repeated in following rows, they are moved one stitch to the right, or one stitch to the left, depending on which side the increase is required.
5. To make a double increase, follow the same instructions, but work three stitches instead of two into the foundation stitch.

Decorative increasing

Make a more decorative increase the following way. Mark the place where the increase is to be made on the wrong side of the work. Then, working on the wrong side, make one chain before the marker if you want the increase to be to the left, or after the marker if you want it to be to the right. On the next row (right side) work the increase stitch into the chain made on the previous row.

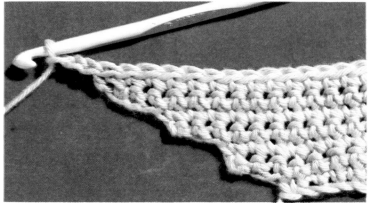

2. Increasing with a chain

3. Increasing to the right. This is made by marking the position for increasing, and working two stitches into one to the right of the marker

4. Increasing to the left. This is made by marking the position for increasing, and working two stitches into one to the left of the marker

1. Increasing by working two stitches into one. This is the simplest method, and can be worked at either end of a row

5. Double increasing. This is the same method as for single increasing, but three stitches instead of two, are worked into one

Decreasing

To decrease one stitch at the side edge, skip the first stitch at the beginning of the row and insert the hook into the second stitch. Work to within the last two stitches in the usual way, skip the next stitch and insert the hook into the last stitch.

To decrease several stitches, work the row and turn, leaving the stitches to be decreased at the end of a row, unworked.

6. There is a way to avoid ugly steps in your work where several stitches have to be decreased at once. For example, if three are to be decreased, work along the row to the last three stitches, skip the next two and work one slip stitch into the last stitch: turn with one chain, skip the slip stitch, work a single crochet into the next stitch, and then continue along the row in the normal way.

Decreasing a stitch in the middle of a row

7. Work two single or double crochet, but keep the last loop of each stitch on the hook. Then draw a loop through all the loops that are remaining on the hook.

Marking position for decreases

When making decreases in the middle of a row, make sure you mark the spot with a length of contrasting colored yarn. Then work the decrease in the two stitches before the marker if it is a right decrease, or in the two stitches after it if it is a left decrease. For example, to decrease on single crochet, insert the hook into the first of these two stitches, yoh, and draw one loop through, keeping it on the hook. Insert the hook into the second stitch, yoh and draw another loop through so that there are three loops on the hook. Then, yoh, draw loop through all loops.

When decreasing or increasing on garments, use the method that gives the neatest edges, as it will be easier to sew together.

6. *Decreasing at the end of a row. This can be worked on either side, producing the slanting edge shown*

7. *Decreasing a stitch in the middle of a row. It is very important to use a marker to keep the decreasing even*

These unusual pillow covers have been made from crocheted diamonds, each made up of two colors and then joined together. This method could be used for anything which is made with squares—a vest, handbag, or an afghan would all look attractive in carefully chosen colors.

Pillows made with colored diamonds

The pillow is made with diamonds crocheted in two colors and then sewn together to form a square. Each square measures 5½ inches square. You can use odd scraps of yarn, but do make sure to choose yarns of similar thickness.

To make a diamond

Work 3 ch.

1st row. Work 2 dc into 3rd ch from hook. Turn. Continue in rows of dc working 3 ch at beg of each row to turn, and inc 2 dc at each end of every row. Work until about 7½ inches wide.

Join contrast yarn with ss and continue, dec 2 dc at each end of every row by leaving last loop of each 3 dc to be decreased on hook, and then drawing yarn through all loops. This decreases 2 dc. Work until 3 dc rem.

Last row. Work 3 dc, leaving last loop of each on hook, then draw loop through all loops on hook.

Work 8 more squares in same manner; sew tog on wrong side.

To make the border

Work 2 rows of sc around edges, working 2 extra sc in each corner st.

Work another side in the same way.

You can, if you like, instead of working two sides, just work one and back it with any strong fabric in a contrasting or blending color. Vary the arrangement of the squares and colors too, to make your very own design.

Transferring your design

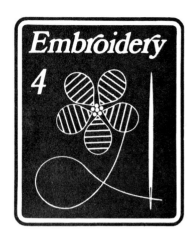

The techique of transferring designs to fabric is one of the key steps in embroidery. When choosing your design, first consider the function of the finished object and also the weaving qualities required of the fabric and threads. You may wish to begin with a small surface such as a table mat, and progress to more elaborate designs. Later Embroidery chapters will describe other methods of transferring designs.

▲ *Ironing on the transfer*

Ironing method

Specially prepared transfers which can be ironed directly onto the fabric are easy to find. There are two types: single impression which can only be used once, and multiprint which gives up to eight impressions, depending on the weight of the fabric (more impressions can be made on a fine fabric than on a heavy one). With both types you have to work on a flat surface.

First establish the center of the transfer by folding it in half lengthwise, then crosswise. Now you are ready to begin. Decide where you want to put the design on the fabric and find the center of your chosen position in the same way. Baste in lines as in adjoining photograph. Match the center of the transfer with the center of the fabric.

Single impression

Cut off any waste lettering from the transfer. Heat your iron to wool setting, and test transfer on a corner or scrap of the fabric you are using by placing the spare lettering face downward and applying the iron for a few seconds. If the transfer takes, you can begin to transfer the design itself.

Place it face downward on the fabric in the exact position you want and pin it at each corner. Protect the fabric not covered by the transfer with tissue paper. Then apply the iron for a few seconds and remove. Lift one corner carefully to see if the transfer has taken. If not, re-iron gently, making sure you haven't moved the transfer or fabric as this will give a double impression.

Multiprint transfers

You can use multiprint transfers in the same way as single impression ones, but with the iron on cotton setting. The only other difference is that if the transfer does not take the first time, you should allow it to cool before re-ironing.

Basting and Tracing methods

If you are working from a drawing, or from any design without a transfer, you have a choice of various methods. The following two are the quickest and easiest to do.

If the design consists of large shapes, basting is the best transferring method. Trace the design onto tissue paper and place this on the cloth, pinning it at each corner. Baste along each line with small running stitches. When you have finished, tear off the paper.

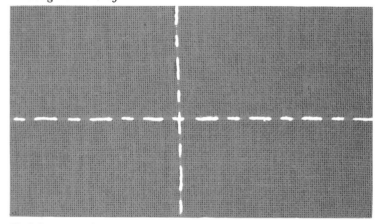

Find the center of the fabric by folding it in half lengthwise and crosswise. Mark with lines of basting.

Tracing designs

By far the quickest and easiest way of transferring designs is to use dressmaker's tracing (carbon) paper. Trace the design onto ordinary tracing paper, then place a sheet of the dressmaker's tracing paper between the design and the cloth, and trace over the design with a sharp pencil.

This method is fine for designs which will be embroidered quickly, but not quite so effective for really large designs because, with constant handling, the tracing on the cloth tends to smudge.

Opposite—transfers, thread and inspiration. Ferns come in all sorts of beautiful graphic shapes—and provide inspiring embroidery ideas for anyone with an eye for design and subtle color. Creative Hands suggests stitches and colors for new ferns in later chapters, but if you would like to give the ferns an individual touch, why not borrow a reference book with color plates of ferns from your local library and interpret your own color schemes? Or, for a more sophisticated effect, you could work them all in gold and silver threads on a cool gray silk background.

Parsley Fern (p. 36).
Cryptogramme crispa.

Pl. 24

69

Snowy owls

This magnificent piece of need-lepoint is made up of 140,700 stitches—worked entirely in tent stitch on single weave canvas with 23 threads to the inch. The work took 300 hours to complete and measures 19 inches by 14 inches.

The picture was designed and worked by Dr. Phyllis Daply, once a surgeon and anes-thetist. Her source of inspira-tion was a couple of photographs taken by Eric Hosking, the well-known bird photographer, on Fetla, one of the Shetland Islands. Dr. Daply patiently interpreted the photographs, and finally pre-sented the masterpiece to Eric Hosking. The realistic appear-ance achieved relies on a clever

use of shading and color tone. Notice particularly the sensitive treatment used to depict the feathers of the owl to the left of the picture, and the smoother texture created by shading on the tree trunk, in contrast to the fluid shading of the many blues in the sea and sky.

If you want to make your own design from a favorite color photograph, the simplest way is to order a big black and white print of the photograph, (which is often expensive) enlarged to the size you want your needlepoint to be. Then, trace off the different tone areas and relate them by numbers to the colors on the smaller color print. Trace these color outlines onto the canvas, and number them as a key to the original.

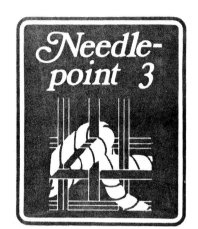

What's in a sampler

The early English samplers which were made from the 15th to the 18th century are fascinating works of art, but in early Victorian days their style became rather uniform and dull. Most of them were worked entirely in cross-stitch or tent stitch, using wool or silk yarns. In America, samplers are also part of the needleworker's heritage. The designs consisted mainly of the alphabet, the maker's name, her age and the date. Later they became more interesting and elaborate, frequently showing family pets and hobbies.

Modern samplers, too, have progressed from a dull repetition of the old designs—as shown by the exciting sampler on the right, which is an adventure in color, texture and pattern. It could be used most effectively as a wall panel, but also looks marvelous as a cushion or tote bag. It is essential with needlepoint to have a practicing ground for each new stitch you learn, and it is a good idea to work two samplers at the same time, one for practicing and one as a clear example of each stitch.

About an inch of the Harvest Fields sampler is missing from the right side of the picture, but if you want to follow the design, the complete pattern is shown in the diagram.

Make a plan of action
Before beginning to make a sampler, decide on a basic plan for the design and color scheme you will use.

If this is your first attempt, you may like to copy the Harvest Fields sampler, shown on the facing page, which has been specially designed for Creative Hands. You may, on the other hand, like to create your own design, but unless you are experienced, try to plan a geometric design and avoid difficult curves.

Copying the design
The chart on the right shows the Harvest Fields design reduced to one third of its actual size. All you have to do is copy the chart, multiplying the measurements by three, onto a larger sheet of plain paper.

Place the copied design securely underneath the canvas and trace in the lines using a ruler and a ball point pen with waterproof ink. This sampler is worked on single thread canvas with eighteen threads to the inch. Make sure when you buy the canvas that it is at least three inches larger than the design. If you've designed your own sampler, you can use any size of canvas, as long as you choose the one most appropriate to the design—coarse canvas for large shapes, and fine canvas for small, intricate ones. A frame is not really necessary for working samplers of this size. Do remember that yarns give texture as well as color, so that it is wise not to use too many colors, or the effect will be muddled. Also, make sure you use enough strands of yarn in the needle because the stitches must cover the canvas fully. Always keep the tension perfectly even so that the design is not distorted.

Yarns and colors
The list below gives the complete range of yarns for the sampler, but if you are planning your own design, you can experiment with unusual yarns as much as you like. Mix silks with wool, or try a fluffy textured wool with the smooth texture of raffia— or make it more exciting with a border of ribbon or beads.

Yarns for the Harvest Fields sampler
Soft embroidery cotton, 6-strand embroidery floss, tapestry wool and crewel wool

Colors for the sampler
3 shades of leaf green
3 shades of olive green
3 shades of golden yellow
2 shades of apricot

You will also need some brown tweed-texture knitting wool and some cocoa-colored plasticized raffia.

Go to town on texture
One stitch for each area is suggested in the diagram, but, of course, you may want to plan your own sampler. Each stitch gives a different texture, so when making a sampler, be sure to arrange the textures in a balanced composition. You can begin by following the easier stitches in the photograph; later chapters of Creative Hands will give directions for the others.

▼ *Scale: ⅓in = 1in of canvas*   *The Harvest Fields sampler* ►

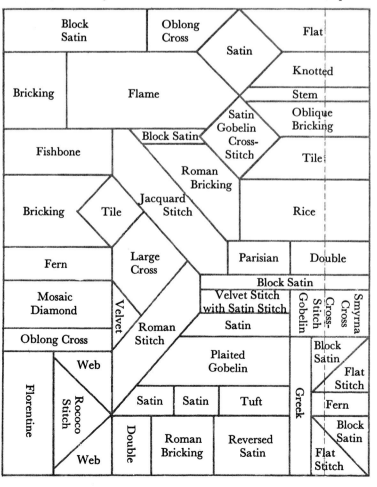

Toy making 1

This bunny's a honey!

Lovable Honeybun is an ideal toy for tiny babies because she is soft and floppy and will not mind being hugged, chewed or tossed around. Light and washable, she is easy to make because the body is all in one piece. The bunny shown is made of pink terry cloth, but if the toy is for a baby boy, blue would look every bit as cute.

What you will need:

- ☐ ¼yd pink terrycloth
- ☐ ½yd 1in wide eyelet embroidery or ribbon
- ☐ Small piece of pale pink seersucker or cotton
- ☐ 6-strand embroidery floss for the features
- ☐ Stuffing. Choose this carefully if you want to be able to wash Honeybun. Dacron fiber is best, but old nylon stockings washed and cut into small pieces are good, as they dry quickly and will not discolor the fabric

How to start

Draw your own pattern pieces on squared paper, using the graph opposite. One square equals 1in square and ¼in seam allowances are included. From the terrycloth, cut out 2 body pieces, 4 ear pieces, 4 arm pieces and 1 foot gusset. From the seersucker, cut out 2 inner ear pieces and 4 hand pieces.

Body

With the right sides facing, pin the two main body pieces to-

74

gether, positioning the foot gusset between the feet.
Baste, then machine stitch all around or hand sew with a firm back stitch. Leave a 3in opening in the middle of the back for stuffing.
Clip the seams at the points marked with a slash on the graph, taking care not to cut too close to the stitching.
Turn to the right side and stuff lightly to form a gently rounded shape. Do not stuff the feet too tightly, or they will stick out sideways.
Sew up the 3in opening with small stitches.

Arms and hands

With the right sides facing, pin, baste and sew the hand pieces together, leaving the wrist end open for stuffing.
Clip the seams where marked, turn to the right side and stuff. Baste across the wrist opening. Now place one hand between two arm pieces, so that the wrist edges are aligned and the fingers point toward the shoulder, as in the diagram. Pin and baste firmly through all four thicknesses and around the rest of the arm.
Sew all around, leaving a 2in opening on one side. Do the same with the other arm.
Turn the arms to the right side and the hands will emerge on the outside.
Push the corners gently into points with a blunt pencil, then stuff and neatly sew up the openings.
Position the top of the arms 5¼in below the top of the head, sewing them to the body at the top of the shoulders.

Ears

Turn under the seam allowance all around the inner ear pieces and baste.
Center an inner ear piece onto two terry ear pieces; slip stitch in place.
Place right sides of ear pieces together, pin, baste and sew, leaving open along the bottom edge.
Turn to the right side, baste the edges, molding the ear into shape, and press.
Remove basting, turn in and sew up the bottom edges, pinching them together to make them slightly rounded.

Firmly sew the ears in the position on the head where they look best.

Face

Embroider the features as shown in the diagrams, using three strands of embroidery floss. Use stem stitch for the eyebrows and the mouth, and satin stitch for the eyes and the nose.

To finish off

Sew the eyelet embroidery around the hem and neck, or trim with ribbon.

Honeybun—a toy which will be loved by children and adults alike!

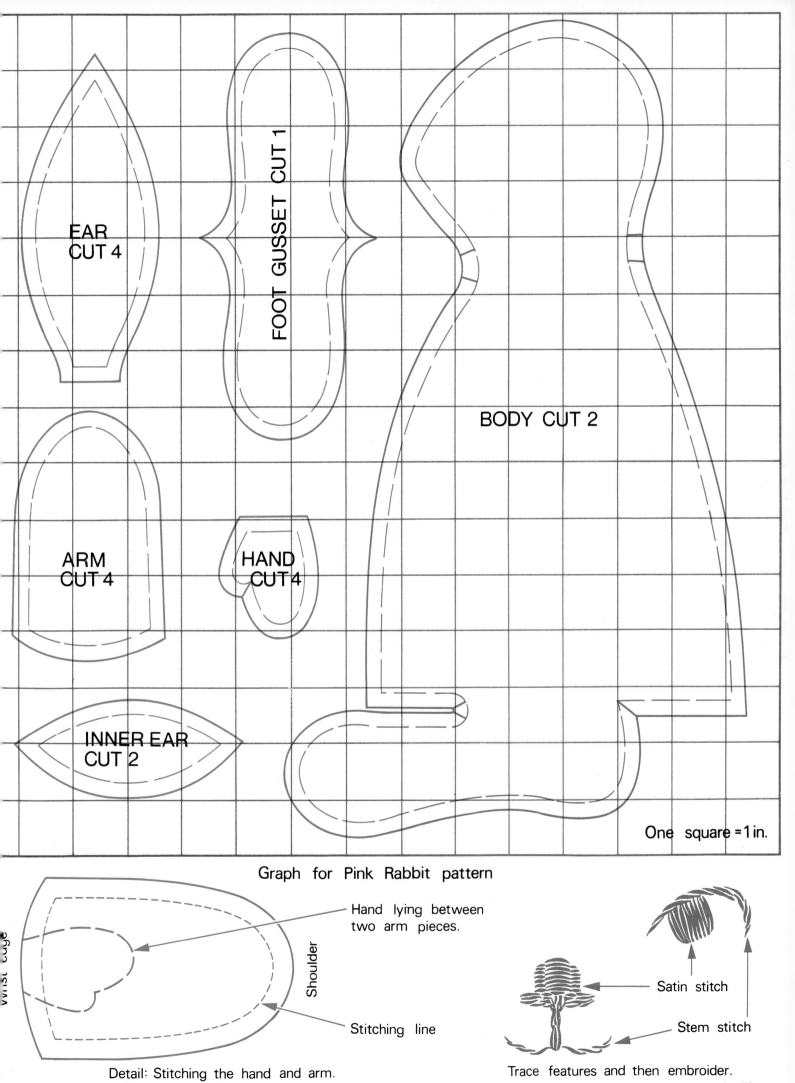

EAR
CUT 4

FOOT GUSSET CUT 1

BODY CUT 2

ARM
CUT 4

HAND
CUT 4

INNER EAR
CUT 2

One square = 1 in.

Graph for Pink Rabbit pattern

Hand lying between
two arm pieces.

Shoulder

Stitching line

Detail: Stitching the hand and arm.

Satin stitch

Stem stitch

Trace features and then embroider.

Theme and variations on a simple skirt

Every one of the elegant skirts shown here can be made from one single pattern, and you can even make that yourself. So instead of having to buy seven different patterns, you simply adapt this one to make the style of skirt you want. The basic skirt pattern is a simple flared style, but in later chapters you will discover how this pattern can be used to make all the variations sketched here. With the length of skirts and the moods of fashion constantly changing, you can be certain that this is one pattern which will go to any length to suit your needs.

What you wear with your skirt is important and demands careful thought, because an unsuitable combination can spoil the effect of any garment. Of course, there is an enormous variety of clothing to choose from for wearing with a skirt, but a collection of blouses provides the ideal answer and gives you the scope to choose the perfect partner for the length and style of skirt you wear.

The blouses sketched here are some variations on the basic blouse from the Creative Hands Dressmaker's Pattern Pack, and instructions for making all of them are given in later chapters. If you make your own blouses and skirts, you can have fun choosing color schemes, and you'll be surprised how many different outfits you can make up if the colors are carefully chosen to match or complement each other and fit in with the rest of your wardrobe.

An introduction to drafting

Making your own pattern may sound like a formidable task, but if you work from a graph, you'll discover it is fun and very easy—in fact, drafting from a graph is the simplest form of pattern making. This chapter starts off with the simple flared skirt, and if you follow the step-by-step instructions carefully, you can't go wrong. Read on and you will see some of the advantages of making your own pattern. The graph is for a 36in hip, 26in waist and 23in length, but you will find the instructions give all the information you need for altering the size of the graph pattern to your own measurements, including full instructions which give the secrets of lengthening and shortening a flared skirt.

Although you will make the pattern to your own size, your individual proportions may not be standard, and you will need to make certain alterations to the pattern. So when you have cut out and basted the skirt, the following chapter describes fitting in detail and shows how to transfer any alterations to the skirt pattern. You will then have an individual pattern which takes all your personal skirt fitting problems into account.

You can use this corrected pattern to make the skirt variations illustrated here. And, because the pattern fits you perfectly, there should be very little fitting to do when you use it again for making up other variations of the basic style.

Theme: the flared skirt...

Straight

4-gore

6-gore

Knife-pleated

Dirndl

Bias-cut

...Variations

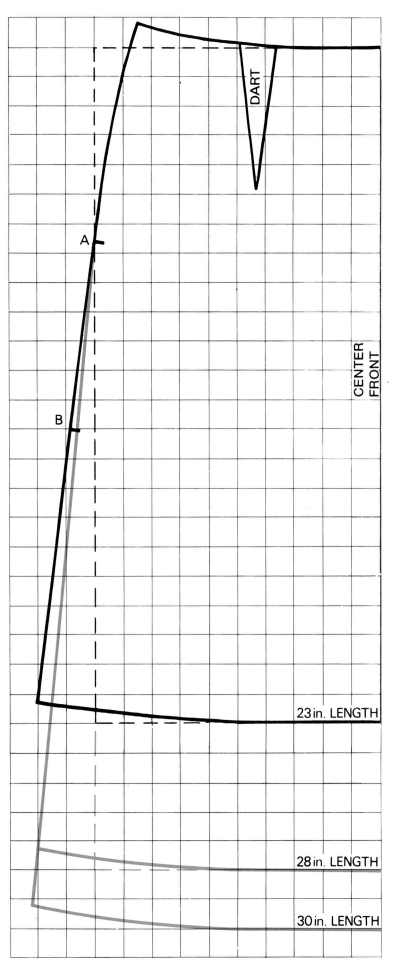

DART

CENTER
FRONT

A

B

23 in. LENGTH

28 in. LENGTH

30 in. LENGTH

Pattern making from a graph

To make the pattern, you will need the following equipment:
☐ Yardstick
☐ Tape measure
☐ Tailor's square, or a 45° set square
   from an art supply store
   will do just as well
☐ Soft pencil
☐ Large sheet of brown wrapping
   paper, with lengthwise
   grain lines

To make a pattern from a graph, just count the squares and translate them into inches. Each square represents one square inch. Here, we use a rectangle of dotted lines to make it easy to obtain the pattern shape, the position of the darts, and the curves. The size of the rectangle is based on the length of the skirt and the hip measurement. The pattern shown on the graph is for size 36in hips and 26in waist. Instructions on changing the size and length of the pattern are given at the end of this chapter, so read first and then take action.

N.B. You do not need to draw the grid squares onto the brown paper, just transfer the outline of the skirt.

How to copy the rectangle and obtain your pattern shape
First, fold the edge of the paper under 1in along the lengthwise grain lines, to give a strong working edge to the center front of your paper pattern. Starting with the black rectangle for the front, count the squares on the center front line of the graph. Measure down 1in from the top and mark in pencil. Then count down for the length of skirt required and mark. Count the squares along the horizontal dotted lines and measure the distance on the paper, making two more pencil marks opposite those on the folded front edge. Connect these points using a yardstick, making this the dotted vertical line, marking it as it appears on the graph.

At this stage, it is very important to double check that the distances between the folded edge and the dotted vertical line are equal, top and bottom, or the pattern will become uneven.

To make the horizontal lines, lay the tailor's square on the folded edge and your first pencil marks, and draw dotted lines across to complete the rectangle.

Make the rectangle for the back skirt section in exactly the same way. These rectangles now give the guide lines to count from, to obtain the pattern outlines, the position of the darts and points A and B (the balance marks). The balance marks are important and have to meet when you stitch the skirt seams together.

For the waistband, mark out a strip 1¼in wide and 13in long, as shown on the graph. This is half your waist measurement. For the waistband to fit snugly, no ease is allowed.

How to alter the graph size
If the size on the graph is too small for you, it is quite easy to increase it. This is how to do it.

Make the patterns as before, but instead of making the fold along the center front edge of your paper 1in, increase the fold to 2in. Next, refer to your measurement chart in chapter 2 for your waist and hip measurements, remembering to add the necessary ease to your own measurements.

Then divide the difference between your measurements and those

◄ *Graph pattern of skirt front for size 36in hip, showing 23in length in black, and 28in and 30in lengths in red. Each square = 1 square inch*

on the graph by eight (this is because you are working on half sections of the pattern only). For example, to increase the pattern to a 40in hip and a 30in waist, you will have to add 4in to the graph pattern size—4in divided by eight means that you will have to add ½in to each center line and side seam. To add ½in to the center lines, unfold the edge of the paper by this amount. To add ½in to the side seams, measure outward from the given line and draw a new line. Make sure that the point where side seam and waist seam meet stays the same distance from the upper horizontal line of the rectangle.

You can reduce the size of the pattern using the same technique, but subtracting at the center lines and side seams instead of adding.

How to alter the graph length

The graph pattern shows a 23in length skirt in black and 28in and 30in lengths in red.

To increase the length to 28in or less the rectangle is increased to the desired length and the pattern made as before. This gives the same flare at the hem as in the shorter version.

For lengths over 28in the flare needs to be increased. To do this, first draw up a skirt 28in long as above. Then extend the line of flare by the required length as shown for the 30in length skirt. If you want to shorten the skirt, it is not necessary to alter the flare.

Cutting out the pattern

You are now ready to cut out the pattern. Before cutting out, be sure that you have marked the folded edges, center front and center back, and balance marks. Cut around all the shapes—cut into the darts, too. It is best to transfer this pattern onto stiff white paper (from an art supply store), since the original will be used later to obtain all the outlines for the other skirt styles you will make.

Fabric requirements

In the next chapter you will be cutting out your skirt. Here is how to calculate the amount of fabric you will need, depending on the width you have chosen.

54in width—for sizes 34½, 36 and 38in hips: your skirt length, measured over side hip, plus 8 inches for seam and hem allowances and waistband.

For 40, 42 and 44in hip: one-and-a-half times your skirt length, measured as above, plus 8 inches.

36in width—twice your skirt length, measured over side hip, plus 11in for seam and hem allowances and waistband.

Choosing your fabric

Having made the pattern and worked out the yardage requirements, it is time to choose your fabric and get everything ready for cutting out.

When choosing fabric, make sure it's easy to work with and practical to wear. When you buy, make sure you ask for skirt or suit weight cloth. Choose from any of the following:

☐ Firmly woven worsted woolens, cottons and linens
☐ Fine grain tweeds
☐ Firm man-made fabrics like acrylics
☐ Mixture fabrics such as wool or linen, which have been blended with nylon, acrylics or polyesters
     You will also need:
☐ Sewing thread
☐ Hooks and eyes
☐ 7in zipper
☐ 1yd stiff grosgrain ribbon or belting 1in wide

Graph pattern of skirt back for size 36in hip showing 23in length in black, and 28in and 30in lengths in red. Each square = 1 square inch ▶

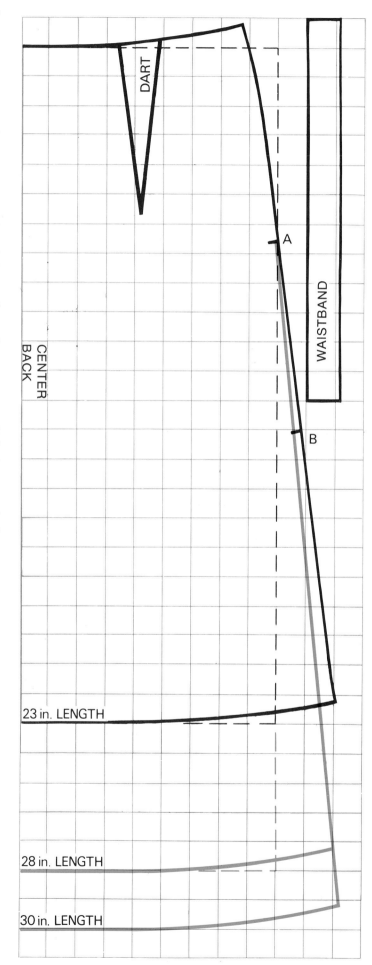

Fashion Flair

Quick-sew cover-up

You will need

Unlined shawl
- ☐ 1¾ yards 36 inch fabric
- ☐ Matching sewing thread
- ☐ 3 tassels (from a trimmings department)
- ☐ 4 yards ribbon at least 2 inches wide.

Suitable fabrics. Fine wool, tweed, heavy silk, wool jersey, georgette, crepe, chiffon, fine silk, voile.
If the fabric is patterned, be sure that the pattern is as pleasing on the wrong side as it is on the right side.
If the material is very lightweight, choose a lightweight ribbon and do not use the tassels.

Lined shawl
- ☐ 1¾ yards 36 inch fabric
- ☐ 1¾ yards lightweight lining
- ☐ Matching sewing thread
- ☐ 2½ yards fringe

Suitable fabrics. Wool and cotton or synthetic mixtures, velvet, fine wool, lace, heavy silk.

Making the shawls

The pattern. Make the paper pattern from the graph. Rule a piece of paper 3ft square into a grid of 4in squares. Copy the

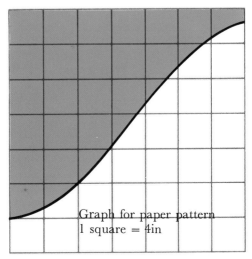

Graph for paper pattern
1 square = 4in

pattern from the graph onto this grid, one square on the graph being equal to one square on the grid.
Cut out the pattern.
The unlined shawl. Pin the pattern onto the folded fabric as shown (figure 1).

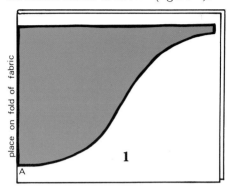

place on fold of fabric

1

A

Cut out the shawl and mark point A with a pin.
Fold the ribbon in half (figure 2) and pin the ribbon over the raw edges of the shawl. Stitch the ribbon in place.

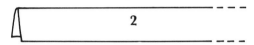

2

Sew a tassel onto each corner and at point A (figure 3).

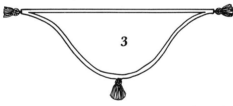

3

The lined shawl. Cut out the fabric for the shawl and the lining as for the unlined shawl.
With right sides together, pin the lining to the shawl fabric and machine stitch around the edges, leaving an opening at point X (figure 4).

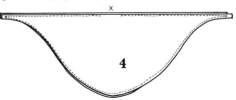

x

4

Turn right sides out and slip stitch the opening closed.

Trimming
Either sew a fringe around the curved edge.
Or sew on three tassels.
Or sew on lace edging.
Or sew little bows at one inch intervals along the curved edge.
Or sew lace daisies into each corner.

Pattern Library

Cross-stitch design

You can use this bold peasant design in many ways. Work a single motif on a table mat, napkin or tray cloth. Arrange the motif in groups to form larger designs for cushions or dress embroidery, or work a handsome border in glowing colors around the hem of a table-cloth. The design is ideal for needlepoint, too.

Thread: D.M.C. 6-strand embroidery floss, 666, 989, 825, 739, 402, and 3371.

Fabrics—you can use any even-weave fabric you like, but the material used here is Hardanger fabric with 18 double threads to 1in. On this material, using 6 strands of cotton throughout and a tapestry needle size 21, the motif will measure about $3\frac{1}{4}$in square. If you use a finer fabric, the design will, of course, work out smaller.

Stitches—work the design in cross stitch throughout over 2 double threads each way, or for single weave fabric, over 4 threads each way.

Knitting Know-how 5

Making patterns from purl and knit

Once you have learned to knit and purl, these stitches can be combined to make a wide variety of decorative patterns, as you can see from the illustrations on the opposite page. The best way to try out these simple stitches is by knitting squares. If you don't have any left-over scraps of yarn, buy several colors in the same ply—knitting worsted is best. A good size for the squares is 4 inches, but you can make them larger or smaller as long as they all measure the same. Besides giving you experience, squares have a number of practical uses. For example, you can sew them up into a pillow case or decorative afghan. Or use them to make any garment where you want a patchwork effect. This chapter will show you how to make a smooth edge on a piece of knitting, so your squares will be neat and easier to sew together.

1. Edge stitch

You'll find that the edges of your work are neater, and therefore more easily sewn together, if you slip the first stitch and knit the last stitch of each row. This is particularly the case in stockinette stitch, where the ends of rows tend to be loose. Knitting the last stitch of every row tightens this edge and gives a smooth finish.

Edge at the end of row

2. Broken rib

Cast on a number of stitches divisible by 4, plus 1.
1st row. *K2, P1, K1, rep from * to last st, K1.
2nd row. *P1, K3, rep from * to last st, P1.
Rep these 2 rows for length required.

Broken rib

3. Rib (1 and 1 rib, or single rib)

Cast on an even number of stitches.
1st row. *K1, P1, rep from * to end.
Rep this row for length required.

4. Rib (2 and 2 rib, or double rib)

Cast on a number of stitches divisible by 4.
1st row. *K2, P2, rep from * to end.
Rep this row for length required.

5. Seed (or moss) stitch

Cast on an odd number of stitches.
1st row. K1, *P1, K1, rep from * to end.
Rep this row for length required.

6. Twisted stockinette stitch

This looks much like stockinette stitch, but has an added twist, made by knitting into the back of the stitch on all K rows.
Cast on any number of stitches.
1st row. K into back of all stitches.
2nd row. P.
Rep these 2 rows for length required.

7. Double seed (or moss) stitch

Cast on a number of stitches divisible by 4, plus 2.
1st row. K2, *P2, K2, rep from * to end.
Rep this row for length required.

8. Basket stitch

Cast on a number of stitches divisible by 8.
1st row. *K4, P4, rep from * to end.
2nd, 3rd, and 4th rows. As first row.
5th row. *P4, K4, rep from * to end.
6th, 7th, and 8th rows. As 5th row.
These 8 rows form the pattern, and are repeated as required.

▲ 3. Single rib

▲ 5. Seed (or moss) stitch

▲ 4. Double rib ▼ 6. Twisted stockinette stitch

▲ 7. Double seed (or moss) stitch ▼ 8. Basket stitch

Striped pullovers

The striped pullover is a basic sportswear item. Directions are here for two versions of this classic garment.

Sizes

Directions are for size 12
Length to center back, 20¾ [21¼:22:22½]in
Sleeve seam, 6[6:6½:6½]in
The figures in brackets [] refer to sizes 14, 16, and 18 respectively.

> ### Gauge
> 6 stitches and 8 rows to 1 inch worked on No. 5 needles.

Materials

Sports Yarn
Pullover A 5 [6:6:7] 2oz balls of main color, A
1 [1:1:1] ball of contrast, B
1 [1:1:1] ball of contrast, C
1 [1:1:1] ball of contrast, D
One pair No.3 needles or Canadian No.10
One pair No.5 needles or Canadian No.8
Set of 4 No.3 double-pointed needles
Set of 4 No.5 double-pointed needles. Stitch holder.
Pullover B 2 [3:3:3] balls of main color, A
2 [2:2:2] balls of contrast, B
1 [1:2:2] balls of contrast, C
One pair No. 3 needles or Canadian No.10
One pair No.5 needles or Canadian No.8
Set of 4 No.3 double-pointed needles or Canadian No. 10. Stitch holder.

Pullover A (back)

Using No.3 needles and color A, cast on 142 [150:158:166] sts. K2 rows.
Change to No.5 needles.
1st patt row *K2, P2, rep from * to last 2sts, K2.

2nd patt row *P2, K2, rep from * to last 2sts, P2.
These 2 rows form patt and are rep throughout.
Continue in patt until work measures 5in, ending with a 2nd patt row.
Keeping patt correct, work in stripes as follows:

1st-6th rows	with C.
7th-10th rows	with A.
11th-14th rows	with B.
15th-16th rows	with A.
17th-18th rows	with C.
19th-22nd rows	with D.
23rd-24th rows	with C.

Continue in patt with A only until work measures 13 [13½:13½:14]in, ending with a 2nd patt row.

Shape armholes

Bind off 8sts at beg of next 2 rows.
Keeping patt correct, dec one st at each end of every row until 106[112:118:124]sts rem.
Continue without shaping until armholes measure 7 [7:7½:7½]in, ending with a 2nd patt row.

Shape shoulders

Bind off 10 sts at beg of next 4 [4:6:6] rows and 11 [13:5:7]sts at beg of next 2 rows.
Leave rem sts on holder.

Front

Work as for back until armholes measure 5in, ending with a 2nd patt row.

Shape neck

Next row patt across 43 [45:47:49] sts, bind off 20[22:24:26]sts, patt to end.
Work right shoulder on these sts. Dec one st at neck edge

every row 12 times.
Work until armhole measures same as back to shoulder, ending at armhole edge.

Shape shoulder

Bind off 10sts at armhole edge every other row 2 [2:3:3] times. Work 1 row.
Bind off rem 11 [13:5:7]sts.
With WS of work facing, attach yarn to rem sts and work to correspond to other shoulder.

Sleeves

Using No.3 needles and A, cast on 86 [86:90:90]sts. K2 rows. Change to No.5 needles.
Work in patt as for back, inc one st at each end of 5th and every following 6th row until there are 98 [98:102:102]sts. Continue without shaping until sleeve measures 6 [6:6½:6½]in.

Shape cap

Bind off 8sts at beg of next 2 rows.
Keeping patt correct, dec one st at each end of every RS row until 24sts rem. Bind off.

Finishing

Steam lightly, not touching garment.
Join shoulder, side and sleeve seams. Sew in sleeves.

Collar

Using set of 4 No.3 needles and A, with RS facing, pick up and K96 [100:108:112]sts evenly around neck. Divide on 3 needles. Work around in K2, P2 rib for 2in.
Change to set of 4 No.5 needles. Continue in rib until collar measures 4in.
Work in stripes as follows:

1st-2nd rounds	with B.
3rd-4th rounds	with A.
5th-6th rounds	with C.
7th-8th rounds	with D.
9th-10th rounds	with C.
11th-14th rounds	with A.

Bind off in rib.

Pullover B (back)

Using No.5 needles and A,

cast on 104 [110:116:122]sts.
1st patt row P2, *K4, P2, rep from * to end.
2nd patt row K2, *P4, K2, rep from * to end.
These 2 rows form patt and are rep throughout.
Keeping patt correct work in stripes as follows:

1st-12th rows	with A.
13th-24th rows	with B.
25th-28th rows	with A.
29th-38th rows	with B.
39th-48th rows	with C.
49th-50th rows	with B.
51st-58th rows	with C.
59th-68th rows	with A.* *
69th-76th rows	with B.
77th-78th rows	with C.
79th-86th rows	with B.
87th-92nd rows	with C.
93rd-94th rows	with B.
95th-96th rows	with A.* *

Shape armholes

Working with A, bind off 6sts at beg of next 2 rows.
Keeping patt correct, dec one st at each end of every row until 78 [82:86:90]sts rem.
When 12 rows in A in all have been completed, change to C and work 8 rows.
Working with A only, continue without shaping until armholes measure 7 [7:7½:7½] in, ending with a 2nd patt row.

Shape shoulders

Keeping patt correct bind off 6sts at beg of next 6 rows.
Bind off 3 [4:5:6]sts at beg of next 2 rows.
Leave rem sts on holder.

Front

Work as for back until 16 [16:18:18] rows in A have been worked after armhole shaping has been completed and last C stripe has been worked.

Shape neck

Next row patt across 31 [32:33:34] sts, turn.
Complete left shoulder on these sts. Dec one st at neck edge every row 10 times.
Continue without shaping until armhole measures 7 [7:7½:7½]in, ending at armhole edge.

Shape shoulder

Bind off 6sts at armhole edge every other row 3 times.
Bind off rem 3 [4:5:6]sts.
With RS of work facing, sl center 16 [18:20:22]sts on holder. Attach yarn to rem sts and work to correspond to other shoulder.

Sleeves

Using No. 3 needles and A, cast on 74 [74:80:80]sts.
Work 10 rows in patt as given for back.
Change to No.5 needles.
Work in stripes as given from ** to ** for patt on back.

Shape cap

Keeping patt correct bind off 6sts at beg of next 2 rows.
Dec one st at each end of next 8 rows.
Change to C for 8 rows, dec one st at beg of each row.
Using A only, dec one st at beg of every row until 20sts rem. Bind off.

Finishing

Steam lightly.
Join shoulder, side and sleeve seams. Sew in sleeves.

Neckband

Using set of 4 No.3 needles and A, with RS facing, pick up and K96 [100:108:112]sts evenly around neck. Divide sts on 3 needles.
Work around K1, P1 rib for 2in.
Bind off loosely in ribbing.
Fold neckband in half to WS and slip st down.

Recommendations for the care of your garment

1. Do not let your garment become excessively soiled.
2. Wash by hand, in lukewarm water with suds.
3. After rinsing, knead out moisture, shape to measurement.
4. Do not place wet garments in strong light or near excessive heat.
5. Steam lightly, not touching garment.

Pullover B left, and pullover A right

Making neat work of joins

Crochet Know-how 5

Before making anything of any size in crochet, you must know how to join yarn neatly and securely. When there are only a few inches of yarn left, lay the end along the top of the stitches still to be worked. Work the next stitch with the new yarn and continue for several stitches over both ends until they are secure. Join the new yarn with a slip stitch, and work the chain to form the first stitch.

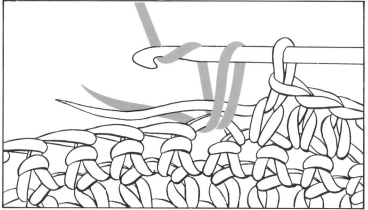

Joining in the yarn

Crocheting into spaces (sps)

When following a pattern, it is often necessary to work into a space made in the previous row, instead of working into or around the stitch. The illustration shows how two stitches have been skipped and 2 chains worked in their place. In the row which has just been started, two stitches are to be worked into the space made by the 2 chains in the previous row.
The usual abbreviation for space is sp.

The traditional American Granny square

Afghan squares are fun and easy to do

An afghan is the name given to a knitted or crocheted blanket or coverlet. These are often made in strips or sections for easy handling, then put together when all the sections are complete. The beautiful afghan shown on the opposite page is made of small squares crocheted in a traditional, much-used design called the American Granny design.

It is common to use odd lengths of wool or left-over scraps of any color for making afghans, but if you have to buy wool, the afghan can take on added sophistication by having a planned color scheme. Choose one color for the background or main color, and two or more colors to tone or contrast. Arrange the finished squares at random as in the illustration, or in lines, or in squares of color for a neat, symmetrical design.

How to make a Granny square
Use 2 different shades of yarn.
With first color, ch4 and join with a ss to form a circle.
1st round. Ch3, 2dc into circle, ch 1, * 3dc into circle, ch 1; rep from * twice. Join into 3rd ch with ss. Break off yarn.
2nd round. Join 2nd color into last sp with a ss, ch2, 2dc into same sp, ch 1, 3dc into same sp, ch 1, * 3dc, ch 1, 3dc, ch 1 into next sp; rep from * twice. Join into 3rd ch with ss. Break off yarn.
3rd round. With first color, join into last sp with ss. Continue working groups of 3dc, with ch 1 between, along sides; and 2 groups of 3dc, with ch 1 between, into each corner.
Work 3 more rounds in same manner, alternating colors.
When squares are ready to be joined, sew them together on one side.
Finish ends by darning into same color yarn so that it is invisible. Either side of the crochet can be treated as the right side.

◄ *Working into a space*

The color scheme for this richly blended afghan was taken from the colors seen in a harbor in Malta, where these pictures were taken ►

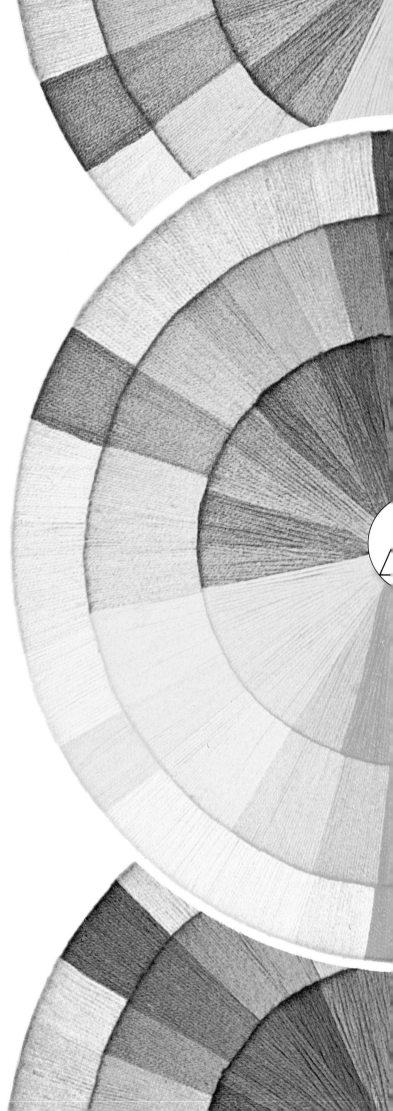

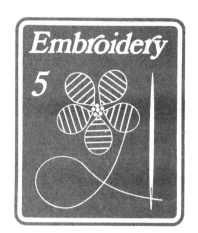

Planning a color scheme

Embroidery 5

A well chosen color scheme can make all the difference between a good piece of embroidery and a really beautiful one. This chapter gives some general principles to follow, but there is plenty of scope for individual taste within them. The colors you choose can be based on natural objects like flowers, stones, shells, or even a transient moment of beauty like the soft blue-grays, pinks and oranges of a sunset. You could take the colors from a dress fabric, or use the colors from a Renaissance painting. The sources of inspiration are endless—just keep your eyes open.

It is very easy to get confused when talking about color, so here are the key terms to make it easier to understand.

Primary colors—red, blue and yellow, at the three points of the central triangle.

Secondary colors—any mixture of two primary colors.

Tone is the light to dark range of a color.

Shade is the darker tones of a color, i.e. mixed with black.

Tint is the lighter tones of a color, i.e. a color mixed with white.

Planning a color scheme

The easiest way to plan a color scheme is to iron the transfer (if it is a multiprint) onto a sheet of paper, and try out colors with crayons, or by laying on pieces of colored paper or thread.

Color schemes are most successful if you use an odd number of colors. Look at a flower, and you will find that it usually has an odd number of colors (3, 5, or 7)—one dominant, one in very small amounts, and any others in fairly equal quantities.

One-color schemes depend upon stitch and texture for effect.

Two-color schemes work best with one light and one dark color, or two clashing or vibrating colors. But always be sure to use more of one color than the other.

In three, five and seven-color schemes use unequal numbers of light and dark colors, even if your design is built up of closely related tones of one color.

Shaded yarn

Shaded, 6-strand embroidery floss is dyed so that the colors vary from light to dark tones of one color throughout the skein. The wings of the pale blue and copper butterfly on the right have been worked to make good use of the dark tones in the center, running out to the lighter tones at the edge of each wing.

A butterfly makes a first-class motif for trying out colors and stitches. You can trace these simple outlines straight from the page and make a couple of butterflies flutter onto a scarf, hover on the sleeve or hem of a little girl's dress, or settle on a pocket. Either look up pictures of real butterflies to find color scheme inspiration, or invent your own scheme with the help of the color wheel.

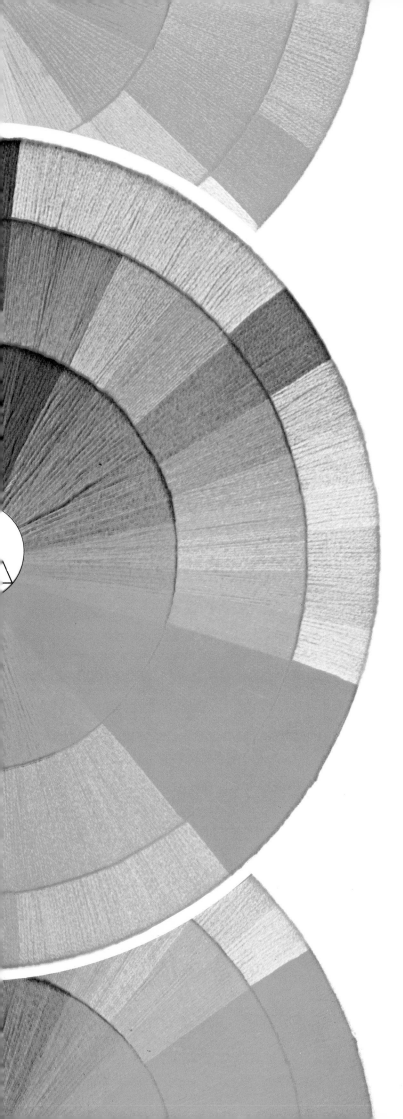

Use of the color wheel

Here are four ways to use this color wheel. Do remember though, a color includes all tones of that color.

1. Use several tones of the same color for subtle, harmonious schemes.

2. Use colors opposite each other for maximum-contrast schemes. These colors vibrate.

3. Use colors at the three corners of an equilateral triangle for rich harmony.

4. Use four colors from one half of the wheel, and a fifth color from the other half.

1. Toned color scheme

Purple butterfly.

Body—satin stitch, violet (three

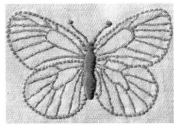

strands). *Wings*—outline: backstitch, lavender (two strands), veins: couching, lavender (one strand).

2. Two-color scheme

Pale blue and copper butterfly—using shaded yarns.
Body—satin stitch, copper (two strands). *Antennae*—stem stitch, burnt copper (one strand).

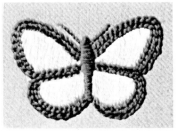

Wings—outline: two rows chain stitch, burnt copper (two strands), inner wings: satin stitch, light blue (three strands).

3. Three-color scheme

Orange butterfly.
Body—satin stitch, lilac (three strands). *Upper wings*—outlined in backstitch, lilac (two strands), filled in shadow work done on wrong side, orange (two strands). *Lower wings*—outlined in four rows of backstitch: outer, lilac (two strands), inner, orange (two strands). *Spots*—outer circles:

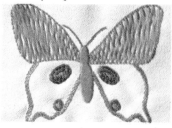

chain stitch, emerald (three strands), and inner contrasting color: satin stitch, lilac (three strands).

4. Five-color scheme

Fantasy butterfly—using magenta and orange as clashing colors.
Body—satin stitch, turquoise (three strands). *Wings*—outlined in chain stitch, magenta

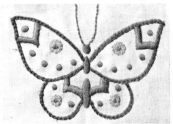

(two strands). *Flashes*—satin stitch, leaf green (three strands). *Small spots*—satin stitch tangerine (two strands). *Large spots*—inner: satin stitch turquoise (two strands), and outer: three rows backstitch, yellow (two strands).

COLLECTOR'S PIECE

Checkerboard Panel

This striking hand-embroidered panel is approximately 12in square. It was inspired by the use of two contrasting fabrics—one plain donkey-gray, the other printed. The plain fabric was chosen in a neutral color to intensify the pinks and mauves of the print. The idea was to link up the printed squares with stitchery reflecting the shapes and colors of the print. A first pattern was formed by arranging printed squares on the plain background and a second pattern was made from the background shapes. Solid pink squares were added to complete the scheme. The deliberate placing of the colored stitchery guides the eye easily from one color to another. Part of each line of stitchery was worked into the pattern on some printed squares. Each color has a varying impact since not every square is covered, nor is every color worked with a shiny thread.

Two stitches are used in this embroidery: simple couching to hold the threads on the surface, and stem stitch. The movement made by the tiny couching stitches when the rows are worked close together adds texture without complicating the pattern.

More stitches for your sampler

Here are some easy and attractive stitches which can be used as groundings or fillings. They also form lovely patterns on their own when worked in two colors or a subtle contrast worked in two tones of one color.

Tent stitch

This is a basic stitch for petit point and is used for gros point when a particularly durable stitch is required. Work from right to left. Come up in the lower left corner of a stitch. Work back over 1 thread (diagonally). Insert the needle, cross behind 2 threads and come up in the new stitch. When the row is complete, turn the work upside down, then work the next row from right to left again. When working over a large area, use diagonal tent stitch to prevent the canvas from being pulled out of shape. The needle is placed horizontally on the row, as shown in the diagram; on the following row, the needle will be placed vertically. The stitch can also be worked in vertical or horizontal lines in alternate directions; when this method is used, it is called reverse tent stitch.

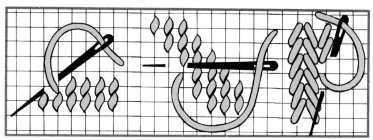

Tent stitch—horizontal, diagonal and reversed

Upright Gobelin

This is worked with straight up-and-down stitches, usually over four horizontal threads of canvas.

Slanted Gobelin

This is similar to upright Gobelin, but worked over 2 vertical and 4 horizontal threads.

Bricking

This upright stitch is worked in interlocking rows.
1st row. Work alternate stitches over 4 horizontal threads.
2nd row. Start 2 threads lower and work a row of stitches over 4 threads, between the stitches of the first row.

Slanted bricking

This stitch is also worked in interlocking rows, but over 2 vertical and 4 horizontal threads, which gives a smooth, slanted texture.

Parisian stitch

This is a small, close, filling stitch worked in interlocking rows over 1 and then over 3 horizontal threads.

Hungarian stitch

Again, this stitch is worked in interlocking rows, over 2 and then over 4 horizontal threads.

Embroider a picture in bricking

The lakeside scene on this page shows how bricking gives faster coverage and more texture to the kind of design where tent stitch is generally used. The bricking is worked in two directions and, if you look closely, you can see that sometimes a 'half brick' or short stitch is needed where two colors or stitch directions meet.
Since every stitch in the picture is so clear, it can easily be copied straight from the page. Always do this kind of two-directional work using single thread canvas, otherwise you will have difficulty in covering the canvas completely.

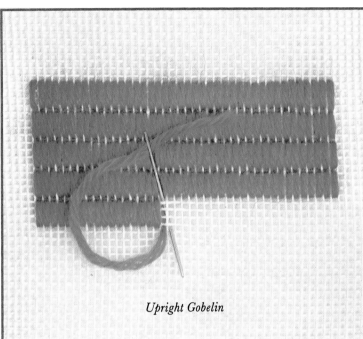

Upright Gobelin

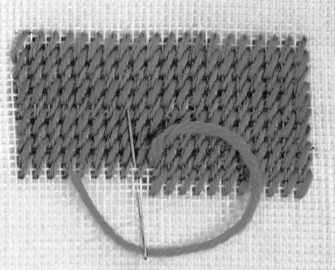

Slanted bricking

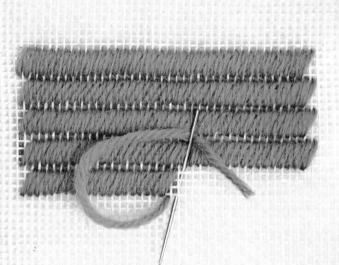

Slanted Gobelin

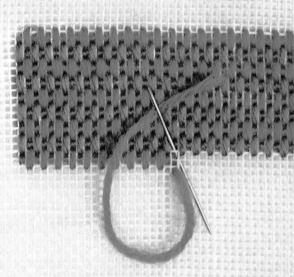

Parisian stitch

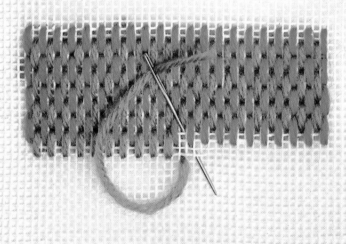

Bricking

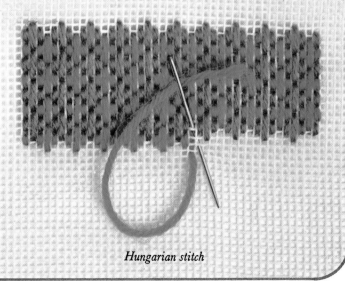

Hungarian stitch

Flounce and filigree

Needle-made lace is very pretty and easy to make. Alpine girls with plenty of time to spare use fine yarn and produce delicate results like the traditional cloth shown below. This particular form of needle-made lace is called Puncetto (pronounced poon-che-toe) and comes from a word in the dialect of Northern Italy meaning stitch. But we are going to present Puncetto in a more modern form which is easier and quicker to make because it is made with thicker threads which give a bold, bright effect.

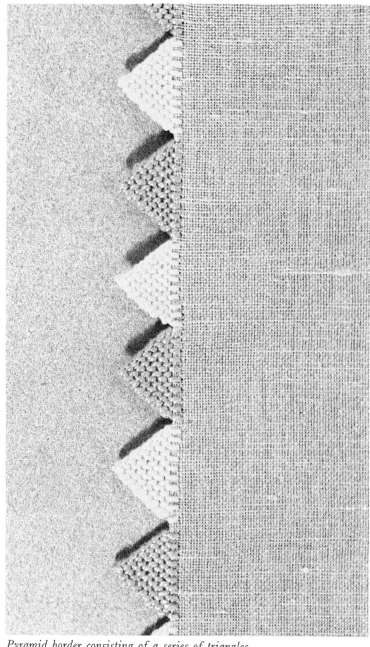

Pyramid border consisting of a series of triangles

Steps to lace-making

Puncetto lace is easy to make. It's simply needle-made knots worked in rows from left to right and back again. You can use it as an edging on a piece of material, or base it on supporting thread. It must always be worked on the right side of the cloth.

Threads to use
Firm, tightly twisted yarns such as fine crochet cotton are best, although for a chunky effect pearl cotton can be used. Of course, the thicker the thread, the faster the work grows.

Use a blunt needle like a tapestry needle.

The basic method
When starting off, hold the material on which the edging is to be worked in the left hand. Work either on a selvage, or make a small hem. Always secure the thread with a couple of tiny backstitches on the wrong side of the work and bring the needle out on the edge. It is most important to keep the stitches of the first row of equal depth and distance from each other, and each knot of uniform tension, or the edging will be spoiled.

First row. Working from left to right, bring the needle upward under the edge of the cloth, two or three threads in from the edge. Take the working thread in the right hand and wind it around the needle once. (Take it from left to right and back, passing it in front of the

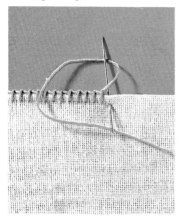

needle first.) Pull the needle up, tightening the knot you've made. Continue in this way making as many knots as required along the edge, taking care to space them evenly.

Second row. Work the second row from right to left. Bring the needle upward through the space between the last two knots of the preceding row. Wind the thread around

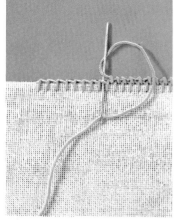

the needle (from right to left and back, passing in front of the needle first) then pull it up, tightening the knot. Continue to the end of the row, keeping the tension even.

Following rows. Repeat the first and second rows as many times as necessary, to make a solid border. Go on practicing this for a while to get the stitches even and then you will be ready to tackle the scalloped,

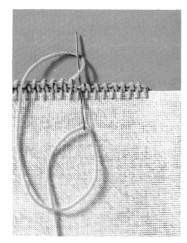

trellissed and other lacy motifs which are to come in later Needle-made lace chapters.

Pyramid border

This simple border consists of a series of triangles which look very pretty edging a baby's pillow, cuffs or a collar. In very coarse thread it makes an unusual and effective edging

for a window shade or lamp-shade. Using the instructions for the basic method, work as many knots as required to form the base of the first triangle and then work back, making one knot less on each row. Continue until the triangle is completed. Then overcast along the side to bring the thread back to the foundation line, ready to start the next triangle.

Needle-made lace has the advantage of being tough and strong, so lends itself to decorating house-hold items. Made with thicker yarns like embroidery cotton, or even colored string, knitting wool or raffia, there are endless possibilities for making lacy things.

Dress-making 5

Preparing to sew the skirt

Having bought your fabric and made the basic skirt pattern from the graph in the previous chapter, you are now ready for the important stages of cutting out the skirt.

Here is the equipment you will need:

☐ Basting thread
☐ Sewing scissors
☐ Tailor's chalk
☐ Pins and needles
☐ Firm table surface

Preparing the fabric

It is essential that the fabric is perfectly smooth before you begin to cut it out. If it has become creased through packing and folding, press the whole length carefully, using a table surface or press board rather than an ironing board. Leave the fabric folded lengthwise with right sides together, and steam the creases out on the wrong side of the fabric using a damp but not wet cloth. Press both sides of the folded length.

Set up your cutting area on a table large enough to take the full folded width and length of the fabric, and fold the fabric as shown in the following layouts and instructions. If you don't want to use a table top, a sheet of hardboard, 4ft wide by 4ft long, will provide you with an excellent cutting surface.

If the fabric is 54in wide, unfold it so that it lies flat on the table. Then, for a hipsize of under 40in, refold the fabric with wrong side out, so that the selvages (finished edges) meet at the center fold line (see layout far right). Smooth out the layers of material toward the new folds to make sure the fabric lies perfectly flat, then secure the selvages to the center crease with pins. For size 40in hip and over, simply fold over the selvages until the pattern width is accommodated (see layout near right).

With narrower fabrics, fold lengthwise, selvages together, smooth out and pin.

Laying out the pattern

Before laying out the pattern pieces, make sure you have marked all pattern details such as center front, center back, and the balance marks on the side seams.

Place the center front and center back lines of the skirt on the fold as shown in the appropriate layout.

Pin both pieces around the edges, making sure they lie flat and are firmly anchored through both layers of fabric.

N.B. Since the pattern is cut without seam or hem allowances, leave enough room around each piece for ¾in seams and a 2½in hem.

Marking the pattern detail on the fabric

Before cutting, transfer the shape of the paper pattern onto the fabric by marking around the edges with continuous tailor's tacks. Once you become more familiar with paper patterns and working on fabrics, you can mark pattern details after cutting.

96

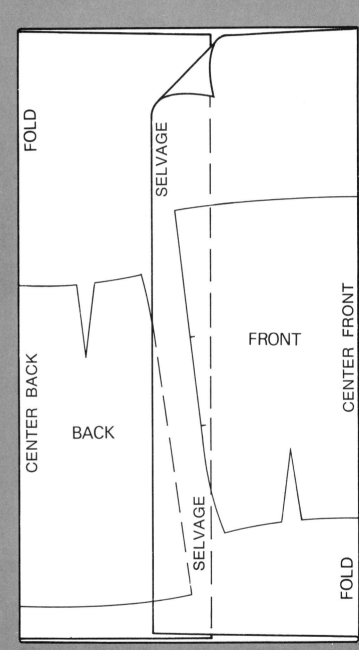

The layout for size 40in hip and over, on a 54in wide fabric

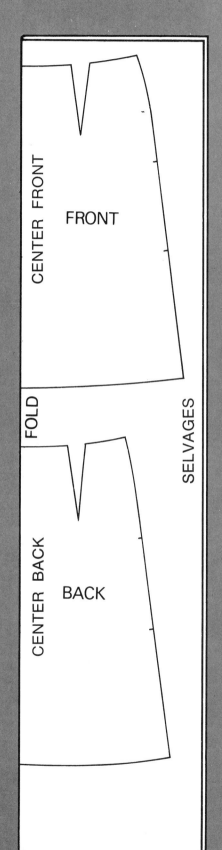

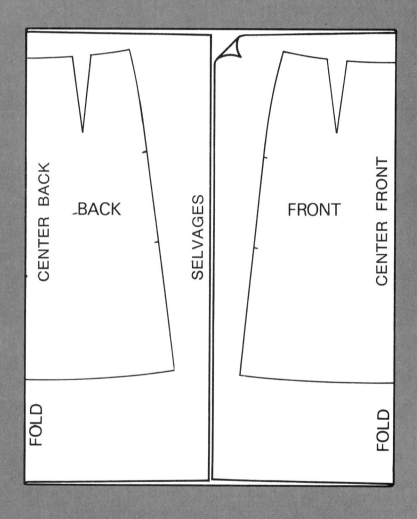

**The layout for sizes 34½,
36 and 38in hip,
on a 54in wide fabric**

**The layout for 36in wide
fabric**

Making continuous tailor's tacks

Thread the needle with basting thread, pulling it through so the ends meet and the thread is doubled. Make the stitches ½in long, leaving a loop about the size of your finger tip on every other stitch as shown.

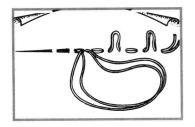

Make tailor's tacks carefully around the pattern and into the **darts**. Work a single tailor's tack to mark the balance marks A and B, using a double thread, and make a back stitch leaving a loop.
N.B. Before cutting, you must add on the hem and seam allowances. Add 2½in for the hem and ¾in for the seams. You can mark these with pins or tailor's chalk. A chalk line is the best method, provided the edge of the chalk is kept sharp by scraping it with a knife, as a thick line can alter the width of your allowances.

Cutting

This is a magic word for even the most experienced dressmakers. It is the point of no return—check once again that all markings and allowances are correct and the fabric is perfectly flat.
Insert the scissors from the top edge of the fabric and cut along your pin or chalk lines with firm, short movements through both layers of fabric. (Do not cut into the darts.) As you cut, keep the paper pattern flat on the fabric and hold it firmly in position with your hand alongside the scissors. This prevents the fabric lifting, which would alter your seam allowance.
After cutting, set aside the remaining fabric which you will need later for making the waistband.
Remove the paper pattern pieces from the fabric.

Separating the layers

Separate the layers of fabric held together by the tailor's tacks by pulling them apart gently along the tacking lines. This will flatten the loops on the top fabric and give enough room to insert the scissors between the layers and cut through the tacks. Be careful when doing this not to cut the skirt fabric.
When you unfold the pieces, the seams and hemline will have a row of tailor's tacks to guide you when you make up the skirt.

Basting for fitting

To baste your skirt together, start with the darts, creasing them down the center, so that both rows of tailor's tacks meet evenly to form a sewing line. Pin. Working from the top edge of the skirt toward the points of the darts, baste them together with small stitches. Use single thread and make flat stitches. Secure ends well with a double backstitch.
Working on a flat surface, place the back and front pieces together with right sides facing and seams coinciding. Make sure the balance marks on the hipline on the back and front correspond and that both layers of fabric lie flat. Pin seams together.
Hold the pinned seams up, and if one side puckers and makes the seam swing out instead of hanging straight, unpin the seam and gently stroke out the fullness. Pin again.
Still working on a flat surface, baste the right side seam. On the left side seam measure 7in down from the waist seam line and leave open for the zipper. Baste the rest of the seam.

The expert touch

After basting the darts and seams, press the seams open with very light strokes, so they will lie reasonably flat for fitting. The importance of pressing as you go can't be stressed enough, because it really does make all the difference.
A complete guide to fitting comes in the next chapter.

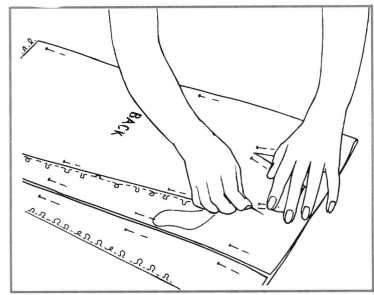

▲ *Marking the stitching line with tailor's tacks*

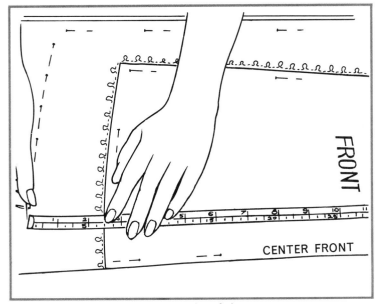

▲ *Marking the hem allowance with a line of pins*

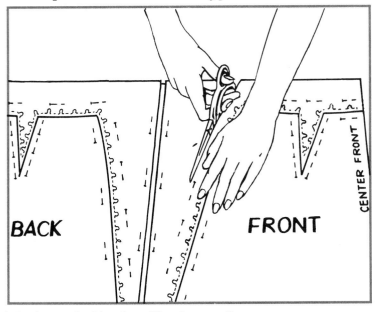

▲ *Cutting out the skirt after adding the seam allowance*

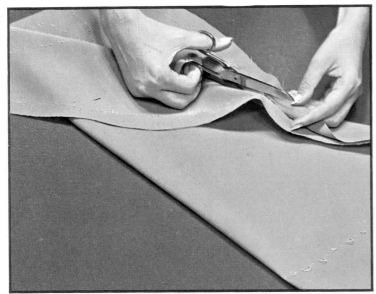

▲ *Separating the layers of fabric by cutting the tailor's tacks*

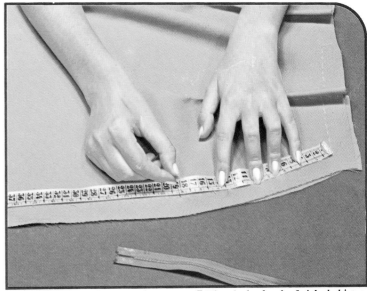

▲ *Measuring the zipper opening*　　▼ *Two looks for the finished skirt*

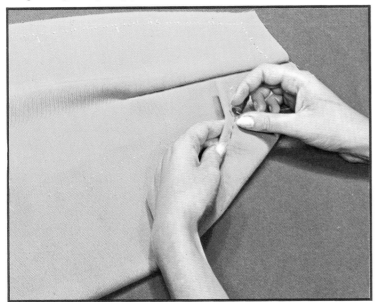

▲ *Basting the darts with small stitches*

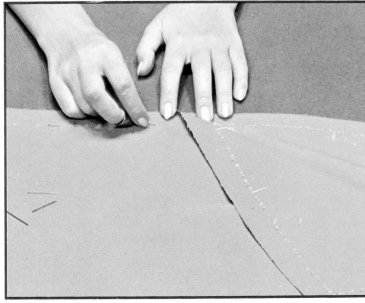

▲ *Pinning the side seams before basting*

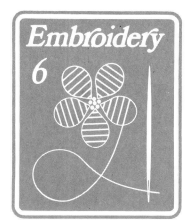

Straight stitches and knots

Once you have a repertoire of straight stitches and knots and know how to transfer designs and choose colors, you are then ready to start filling in shapes. So, why not try your hand at embroidering some of these filling stitches and knots on the beautiful botanical fern designs which are shown on the next two pages?

Satin stitch

Satin stitch is useful for solid fillings, and consists of straight stitches worked evenly and closely together. The illustration below shows how to fill in a leaf shape or a flower center. If you're working this stitch on an article which you use, it is unwise to choose a stitch more than ⅜in long, because it will not wear well. However, if the work is to be mounted as a picture or a wall panel, the stitches may be any length. When using a twisted yarn like pearl cotton, take care to keep it evenly twisted while working. Stranded floss is more difficult to use successfully with satin stitch, as all the strands must lie flat and parallel.

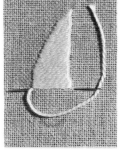 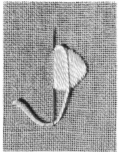 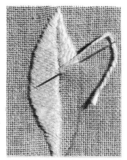

Seeding

Seeding stitches can be used to fill any area and to give a textured effect to a design. This simple filling is made up of many small straight stitches of equal length placed at random. To give greater relief, you can work one stitch over another.

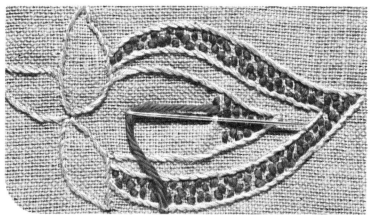

Wheatear stitch

This is a versatile openwork stitch which is ideal for the filigree parts of the first fern, Hermionitis Palmata. Worked in a chain, it looks very like an ear of wheat, from which the stitch takes its name. However, the effect can be changed completely if the stitch is worked in parallel rows.

Work two straight stitches at A and B, bringing the needle through below these stitches at C. Pass the needle under the two straight stitches without entering the fabric, insert the needle again at C, and bring it through at D. (The letters A through D apply to both methods of working the stitch).

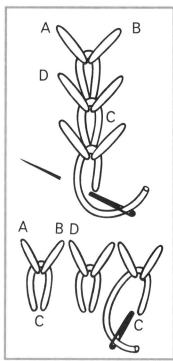

French knot

Bring the needle through to the right side of the material in the required position. Take the working thread in your left hand and wind it twice around the needle. Then, still holding the thread firmly in the left hand, insert it close to where it first emerged. Pull the needle through to the back and secure the knot, or bring the needle up in position for the next stitch. Each stitch should resemble a bead.

Use a thick needle with a small eye so it passes through the coiled thread easily. Choose a

needle size depending on the thread used—a large crewel, or medium chenille for soft embroidery cotton and wool, and a fine crewel for stranded floss.

Bullion knot

Make a backstitch the length of the knot required, but do not pull the needle right through the fabric. Twist thread around the needle point as many times as needed to fill the length of the backstitch. Pull the needle through, holding the left thumb on the coiled thread. Then, still holding the coiled thread, and twisting the needle in the direction indicated, re-insert the needle at the point where it was first inserted. Pull the thread through until the bullion knot lies flat.

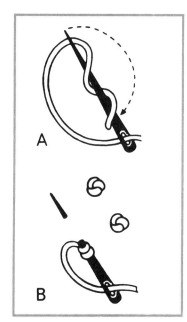

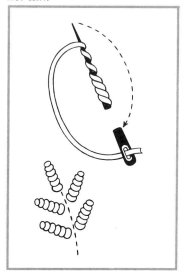

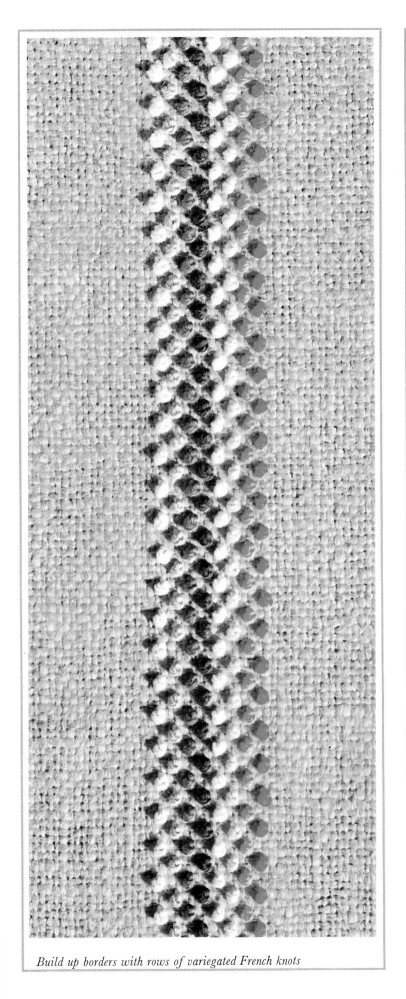

Build up borders with rows of variegated French knots

Bullion and French knots in varying thicknesses of one-color thread

Here is a suggestion for using one of the stitches described in this chapter. The bodice of the dress is worked in outline stitch for the stems and French knots for the little berries.

Ferns and fronds

Here's the modern answer to the Victorian sampler—
a set of eight botanical ferns, specially designed for Creative
Hands so that you can try out the many different stitches
featured in these embroidery chapters. Three of the ferns are
included in this chapter and the remaining ferns in the set
will be given as the new stitches are introduced. Each fern is
suitable for a different set of stitches, clearly indicated on the
outline drawings for you to follow. For instance, the first
fern, Hermionitis Palmata, is designed so that you can
practise straight stitches, parallel wheatear stitch, French
knots and bullion knots. Apart from providing beautiful shapes
on which to practise new stitches, the ferns can be used to make
a set of table mats or as motifs on a table cloth. The complete
set, with the Latin names included, would make a
magnificent botanical wall panel.

Threads and fabrics

The numbers given are colour numbers and refer throughout
to Anchor Stranded Cotton. Use two strands for the best effect.
The colours are those used by the designer and are given as
suggestions but, of course, you may wish to plan your own
favourite colour scheme. The background fabric you use can
be fine embroidery linen, ready-made table mats, or cloths.
If you are making a wall panel, finely slubbed or textured
furnishing fabrics are ideal.

Platyloma Falcata ▶

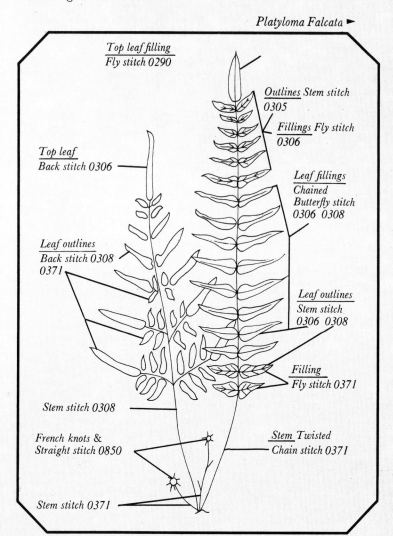

Top leaf filling
Fly stitch 0290

Outlines Stem stitch
0305

Fillings Fly stitch
0306

Top leaf
Back stitch 0306

Leaf fillings
Chained
Butterfly stitch
0306 0308

Leaf outlines
Back stitch 0308
0371

Leaf outlines
Stem stitch
0306 0308

Filling
Fly stitch 0371

Stem stitch 0308

French knots &
Straight stitch 0850

Stem Twisted
Chain stitch 0371

Stem stitch 0371

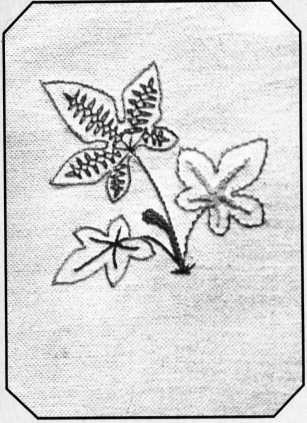

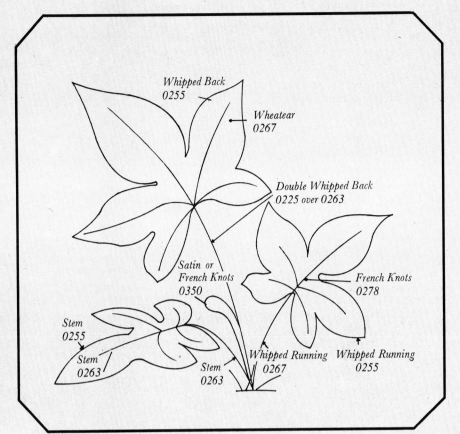

▲ *Hermionitis Palmata* ▼ *Scolopendrium Officinarum*

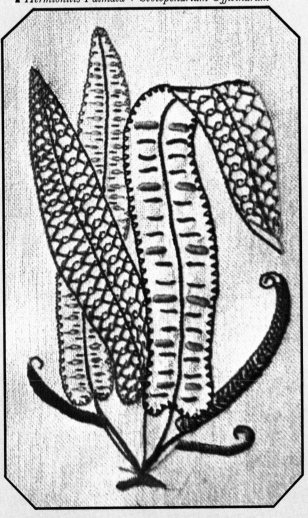

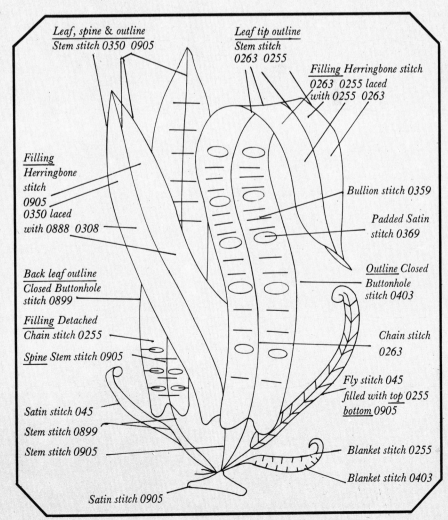

Whipped Back 0255

Wheatear 0267

Double Whipped Back 0225 over 0263

Satin or French Knots 0350

French Knots 0278

Stem 0255

Stem 0263

Stem 0263

Whipped Running 0267

Whipped Running 0255

Leaf, spine & outline Stem stitch 0350 0905

Leaf tip outline Stem stitch 0263 0255

Filling Herringbone stitch 0263 0255 laced with 0255 0263

Filling Herringbone stitch 0905 0350 laced with 0888 0308

Bullion stitch 0359

Padded Satin stitch 0369

Back leaf outline Closed Buttonhole stitch 0899

Outline Closed Buttonhole stitch 0403

Filling Detached Chain stitch 0255

Chain stitch 0263

Spine Stem stitch 0905

Fly stitch 045 filled with top 0255 bottom 0905

Satin stitch 045

Stem stitch 0899

Stem stitch 0905

Blanket stitch 0255

Blanket stitch 0403

Satin stitch 0905

Top and pants for a toddler

If frills and ruffles aren't the style for your baby, then why not crochet this crisp and simple top and pant suit. Make it all in one color, or make it look extra smart with the pants and trimming worked in a contrasting color, say navy with white, or yellow with orange.

Sizes

Directions are for size 6 months.
The figures in brackets [] refer to the 1-year and 2-year sizes respectively.

Gauge
3 'V' groups and 3 rows to 1in.

Materials

7 [8:9] ounces Sports Yarn
1 No.E (3.50mm.) crochet hook, or size required for gauge 4 small buttons
¼ yard elastic

Top front

Ch66 [70, 74] loosely.
1st row 2dc into 4th ch from hook, * skip 1 ch, 2dc into next ch. Rep from * to last ch, 1 dc into last ch. Turn.
2nd row Ch3, * 2dc into next dc, skip 1 dc, rep from * to last dc, 1 dc into 2nd ch of turning ch. Turn. 31 [33, 35] complete 'V' groups.
The 2nd row forms the 'V' pattern and is rep throughout.
Work 3 [4, 5] rows.
Dec at each end of next row by making only 1 dc into first and last 'V' of previous row. This means that in the next row, two less 'Vs' are worked

than before the dec.
Continue patt, dec in this manner at each end of every 6th [7th, 8th] row until 28 [29, 30] rows in all have been worked. 23 [25, 29] complete 'V' groups.

To shape armholes
1st row Ss over 4sts, ch3, work in patt to last 4sts. Turn.
Work 9 [10, 11] rows.
19 [21, 25] complete 'V' groups.

To shape neck
Work 3 rows on 7 [8, 9] 'V' groups. Finish off.
Work other shoulder in same way.

Top back

Work as given for front until armhole shaping row has been completed.
Next row Work across half the sts, turn, and complete one side on these sts, working as given for front.
Finish off.
Attach yarn and work other side in same way.

Sleeves

Ch32 [34, 36] loosely.
Work 3 rows in patt as given. 14 [15, 16] complete 'V' groups.
Inc at each end of next row by adding 1dc to first and last 'V', each of which will become a 'V' in the following row, thus adding 2 'V' groups after inc.
Continue patt, inc each end of every 4th row until 18 [20, 22] rows have been worked.

Shape sleeve cap
1st row Ss over 4sts, ch3, patt to last 4sts. Turn.
Work 8 [9, 10] rows, dec at each end of every alternate row. Finish off.

Front trimming

Ch20.
Work 7 rows sc.
Work corded edge around both long sides, and one short end, as follows—
1 row sc, working from left to right instead of the usual right to left, to give an extra twist to the stitch, and inserting hook under both horizontal threads of the edge stitches.

Pants

Ch48 [52, 56] loosely.
Work in patt as given for Top front for 23 [24, 25] rows.
22 [24, 26] complete 'V' patterns.

To shape crotch
Next row Ss across 15 [17, 19] sts, ch3, work next 8 'V' groups, 1 dc. Turn.
Work 6 rows on central sts.
Next row Work to end. In place of turning ch, ch15 [17, 19] loosely.
Break off the yarn.
At the other end of same row, join yarn and ch16 [18, 20] loosely. Turn.
Work across all sts in patt.
Work 23 [24, 25] rows.
Finish off.

Finishing the top

Join shoulder seams. Sew in sleeves, join the sleeve and the side seams.
Back opening With right side of work facing, beg at base of left side of opening and work 1 row sc evenly up left side, around neck and down right side. Turn and work 2nd row. Mark position for 3 buttons on the left side.
3rd row Work to top of right side, level with first marker* skip 2sc, ch2.
Work in sc until next marker is reached, rep from * until

3 buttonholes have been worked, complete row. Turn.
4th row Work up right side of opening and around neck using sc. Turn.
5th row Work in corded edge st around neck to top of the opening.
Work corded edging around wrists and lower edge.
Sew tab trimming neatly to center front.
Press very lightly with a dry cloth, using a cool iron.
Sew on buttons.

Finishing the pants

Fold in half at crotch. Join side seams.
Work corded edging loosely around leg openings.
Thread elastic through waist edge, and sew ends together to form circle.
Press lightly.

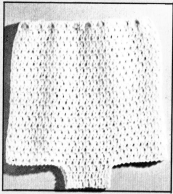

▲ *The matching pants*

Crocheted top for a toddler ►

▼ *Back view of top*

Crochet a vest in squares

You have already seen how to work squares using just two colors in Crochet Know-how chapter 5. The vest design featured here is based on the use of four colors arranged in different combinations in squares of four rounds each. You will need to work sixty two of these, plus two half squares for the front shaping. You can make every square different by varying the number of colors and their sequence in each square. (If you do this, you might chart your plan before you begin.) Or you can simply make each square using the same combination.

For the vest shown, you will need a total of 16 ounces of fingering yarn and a No.D crochet hook. Be sure to remember that if you intend to use one main color as the last round of every square, you will need more of this color in proportion to the three contrasting colors.

The measurements are for a 34-36in bust size, with an underarm length of 17½in. This size is based on a 3½in square, joined together in rows of ten. To vary the bust size, use a different size of hook to work a smaller or larger square. For example, to make a 30-32 in size use a hook which will work a 3in square, ten of which when joined together will give you the size you want. Add extra rows of squares to alter the length of the vest to a sweeping midi worn over flowing evening trousers. Take away one or two rows and you have a snug bolero.

Size
To fit a 34-36in bust.
Length to center back, 24½in.

Gauge
Each square measures 3½ x 3½in worked on No.D crochet hook

Materials
Fingering yarn
4 oz each of 4 colors
One No.D (3.00mm.) crochet hook

To make a square
Ch4. Join with a ss to first ch to form circle.
1st round. Ch3, 2dc into circle, ch2, *3dc into circle, ch2, rep from * twice. Join with a ss to 3rd of first 3ch.
2nd round. Ch2, work 3dc, ch2, 3dc into first ch2 space to form corner, *ch 1, work 3dc, ch2, 3dc into next ch2 space to form corner, rep from * twice. Join with a ss to 1st of first 2ch.
3rd round. Ch3, 2dc into first ch space, ch 1, *work 3dc, ch2, 3dc into corner ch2 space, ch 1, 3dc into next ch 1 space, ch 1, rep from * twice, work 3dc, ch2, 3dc into last corner space, ch 1. Join with a ss to 3rd of first 3ch.
4th round. Ch2, 3dc into next ch 1 space, ch 1, * work 3dc, ch2, 3dc into corner ch2 space, ch 1, 3dc into ch 1 space, ch 1, 3dc into ch 1 space, ch 1, rep from * twice, work 3dc, ch2, 3dc into last corner ch2 space, ch 1, 3dc into next ch space. Join with a ss to 1st of first 2ch. Fasten off.

Make 61 more squares in this way, varying the theme by using only one color or combinations of two, three or four colors.

To make a half square
Ch32.
1st row. Into 3rd ch from hook work 1 dc, 1 dc into next ch, ch 1, skip 1 ch, work 1 dc into each of next 3ch, ch 1, skip 1 ch, work 1 dc into each of next 3ch, ch 1, skip 1 ch, work 1 dc into each of next 3ch leaving last loop of each dc on hook, skip 1 ch, work 1 dc into each of next 3ch leaving last loop of each dc on hook, yoh and draw through all 7 loops on hook, ch 1, skip 1 ch, work 1 dc into each of next 3ch, ch 1, skip 1 ch, work 1 dc into each of next 3ch, ch 1, skip 1 ch, work 1 dc into each of last 3ch. Turn.
2nd row. Ch3, into first ch loop work 3dc, ch 1, skip 3dc, 3dc into next ch loop, ch 1, skip 3dc, work 3dc into next ch loop leaving last loop of each dc on hook, skip corner cluster, work 3dc into next ch loop leaving last loop of each

dc on hook, yoh and draw through all 7 loops on hook, ch 1, skip 3dc, work 3dc into next ch loop, ch 1, skip 3dc, work 3dc into next ch loop, 1 dc in turning ch. Turn.
3rd row. Ch3, into first ch loop work 3dc, ch 1, skip 3dc, 3dc into next ch loop leaving last loop of each dc on hook, skip corner cluster, work 3dc into next ch loop leaving last loop of each dc on hook, yoh and draw through all 7 loops on hook, ch 1, skip 3dc, 3dc into next ch loop, 1 dc into turning ch. Turn.
4th row. Ch3, work 3dc into first ch loop leaving last loop of each dc on hook, skip corner cluster, work 3dc into next ch loop leaving last loop of each dc on hook, yoh and draw through all 7 loops on hook, 1 dc into turning ch. Fasten off.
Make one more half square in the same way varying the colors according to your theme.

Finishing

Darn in all ends. Press each square under a damp cloth with a warm iron. Sew or crochet 10 squares together to form 1 row and join 5 rows in same way (50 squares). To 4 center squares of last row join 2 rows of 4 squares for center back (58 squares). Skip first and last square at end of last row and join 2 rows of 1 square to 2nd and 9th squares, leaving 3rd and 8th squares on last row to form underarm. Join half motif to first and 10th squares of last row to form neck shaping. Join 2nd square to first of 4 center back squares and 9th square to 4th of 4 center back squares to form shoulders. Press.
With RS facing beg at underarm square of lower edge and work 1 round sc up front, around neck, down front and around lower edge. Join with ss to first st. Work around armholes in same way. Press. If you prefer, work a picot edge (see Crochet Know-how chapter 10).

Binding off invisibly

1. *Invisible binding off, working the first two stitches on the row*

Experienced knitters and beginners alike have probably experimented with the special invisible casting on method shown in Knitting Know-how chapter 2. Now Creative Hands introduces you to an equally marvelous technique for invisible binding off. You will also see how to work double casting on, and with both methods you can fashion a ready-made hem with built-in casing for elastic or cords. The depth of the hems can be varied by the number of rows worked.

Although the invisible technique may be a little slower than your usual method at first, don't let this discourage you. For once you have mastered it, you will find that the very professional results are well worth the extra time.

The drawing on the opposite page shows some of the uses for which these invisible binding off methods are most appropriate. For example, you can use them for neck edging, belts and hems; for rib collars, V-necks and round necks.

Invisible binding off

Directions are given for binding off when K1, P1 rib over an odd number of stitches has been used, the first row beginning with K1.

Work the ribbing normally until only 2 more rows are required to give the finished depth or, if a hem casing is required, less the depth of this hem, ending with a wrong side row.

1st row. K1, *ytf, sl 1, ytb, K1, rep from * to end.
2nd row. Sl 1, *ytb, K1, ytf, sl 1, rep from * to end.

Repeat these 2 rows once more, or required number of times to give correct depth of hem.

Break yarn, leaving a length at least three times the length of the edge to be bound off. Thread this into a darning needle. Holding the darning needle in the right hand and the needle with the stitches in the left hand, work throughout from right to left along the stitches on the needle.

1. Insert the darning needle in the first knit stitch as if to purl it and pull the yarn through, then into the next purl stitch as if to knit it and pull the yarn through, leaving both of these stitches on the left-hand needle.

2. *First work 2 of the knit stitches.

Insert the darning needle into the first knit stitch as if to knit it, pull the yarn through it and slip off the needle.

Pass the darning needle in front of the next purl stitch and into the following knit stitch as if to purl it. Pull the yarn through.

3. Now work 2 of the purl stitches.

Insert the darning needle into the purl stitch at the end of the row as if to purl and slip it off the needle.

Pass the darning needle behind the next stitch and into the following purl stitch as if to knit it. Pull yarn through.

Repeat from * until all stitches have been worked off. Fasten off.

2. *Invisible binding off, working the 2nd knit stitch*

3. *Invisible binding off, working the 2nd purl stitch*

Double casting on

When a less elastic cast-on edge is required at the lower edge of a jacket or sweater, the double casting on method is more suitable. Use a short length of contrasting yarn for casting on. This does not become part of the finished work. Using the one needle method, cast on half the number of stitches required.

Using the yarn in which the garment is to be made, begin with a knit row and work 6 rows of stockinette stitch, or the required number of rows to give correct depth of hem casing.

1. Slip the first row of loops which show in the contrast yarn onto a spare needle and pick off the contrast yarn because it is no longer required.

2. Fold the work in half, holding the spare needle behind the other needle, and work both sets of stitches onto one needle in the following way: *K1 from front needle, P1 from back needle, rep from * until all stitches are on one needle.

This may seem a bit awkward, but it does work out.

Continue in rib for required length. If you want to use this edge for a pattern which does not give detailed directions, simply cast on half the number of stitches given. The total number will be made up when the stitches are worked onto one needle.

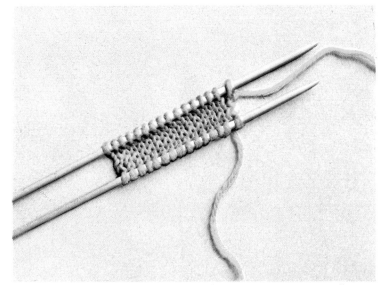

1. *Double casting on—the garment yarn loops put onto a spare needle*

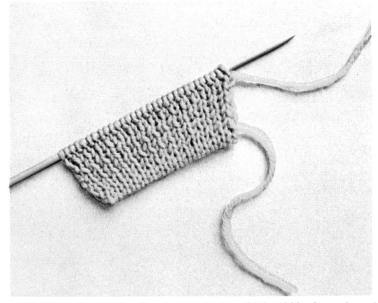

2. *Double casting on, showing the smooth edge with its hidden inner channel*

Fashion Flair

Peasant-style bolero to sew

You will need

- [ ] 1 suede skin about 3ft by 2ft 6in
- [ ] 2yds cord or suede thonging
- [ ] Matching thread
- [ ] Eyelet-setting kit and 8 eyelets (or, any good shoe maker will make the eyelets for you)
- [ ] 3 sheets of brown paper at least 10in by 16in
- [ ] Pencil
- [ ] Ruler
- [ ] Masking tape

Making the pattern

The pattern here will fit bust sizes 34 to 38 inches. The secret is in the lacing! Rule each sheet of paper into a grid of 1 inch squares. Copy the pattern and all the details from the graph on to your grids, one square on the graph being equal to one square on the grids.

Make 2 patterns for the bolero front and 1 for the bolero back. Cut out the patterns.

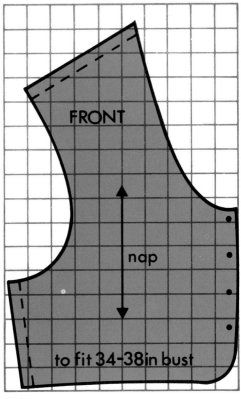

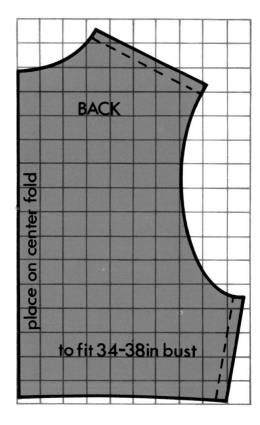

Cutting out

Arrange the pattern pieces on the wrong side of the suede skin. Although there is no grain in suede, there is a nap, so, if possible, try to get all the pattern pieces running the same way.

Stick the pattern pieces down with small pieces of masking tape. This avoids the need for pins, which would mark the suede.

Cut out all the pieces and detach the paper patterns.

Making the bolero

Place the bolero fronts onto the bolero back, right sides facing. Machine stitch them together at the shoulders (Figure 1), using a long stitch and making $\frac{1}{2}$ inch seams.

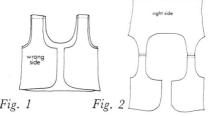

Fig. 1   Fig. 2

Open the bolero and topstitch the seam allowance down on each side of the shoulder seams, $\frac{3}{8}$ inch away from the seam line (Figure 2).

Turn the bolero inside out, join the side seams (Figure 3) and stitch the seam allowances down as before.

Turn the bolero to the right side and make 2 rows of stitching $\frac{1}{2}$ inch and $\frac{5}{8}$ inch from all the edges (Figure 4).

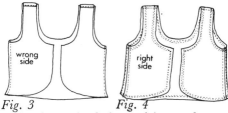

Fig. 3   Fig. 4

Make the eyelet holes and insert the eyelets on both front edges of the bolero using the pattern for the positioning of these holes. You can mark the positions through the pattern with a pencil, as the punch will cut the pencil marks away.

Lace up the bolero with the cord or thonging after you have put the bolero on. You can adjust the lacing according to your bust size.